To: Holly
Poppy Smith
Rom. 14:1

Reaching Higher

Ten Dynamic Truths From Abraham That Will Transform Your Life

By
Poppy Smith

IPG

Intermedia Publishing Group

Reaching Higher
Ten Dynamic Truths From Abraham
That Will Transform Your Life

Published by:
Intermedia Publishing Group, Inc.
P.O. Box 2825
Peoria, Arizona 85380
www.intermediapub.com

ISBN 978-1-935906-12-4

By Poppy Smith

I'm Too Young to Be This Old!

I'm Too Human to be Like Jesus

Wisdom for Today's Woman:
Insights from Esther Bible Study

Speaking Wisely: Exploring the
Power of Words Bible Study

May God use this book
to encourage, comfort,
and spur you on to live a life
worthy of Him.

POPPY SMITH is the author of *I'm Too Young to Be This Old* and *I'm Too Human to be Like Jesus*. She was a Bible Study Fellowship lecturer for many years and is a popular speaker at retreats, conferences, and workshops around the world. Born in England, she has lived in Sri Lanka, Singapore, and Kenya, where she met her American physician husband. They have two grown children.

You can contact Poppy at:

16124 NW St. Andrew's Drive
Portland, OR 97229
poppy@poppysmith.com
www.poppysmith.com

Acknowledgments

To David Sanford, author, agent, friend, my deep thanks for your encouragement. My thanks also to my writing mentor and sage advisor, Connie Soth, for teaching me so much. In addition, I thank my husband, Jim, for his willingness to take on chores he never expected to do so I could be free to write. You are a gem!

Contents

One

View Life as an Adventure

A Remarkable Experience

"*I*'m going to climb Kilimanjaro with some friends in a couple of weeks. Would you like to go with us?" asked Jim, my boyfriend. When you live in Nairobi, Kenya, Mt. Kilimanjaro is a five-hour drive away. Soaring 19,000 feet above the African plains, its snow-covered peak attracts adventure-seekers from around the world. Jim wasn't about to miss his chance.

Gulping, I cautiously replied, "Uh, yes, but I've never climbed a mountain in my life. In fact, the only climbing I've ever done is up three flights of stairs to my office."

"Don't worry," said Jim cheerfully. "You'll do fine. It's only a long walk—three days up and two down. Plus, we have porters to carry everything and huts to sleep in. I'll let Bob and the others know you'll be joining us."

Wondering what had possessed me to say yes, I began to think about several issues of vital importance to most women: What would

I wear? What would Jim's American friends think of me, his so young and so very English girlfriend? And—were there rest rooms along the trail, or did you have to hope for strategically placed bushes?

Based on my meager exposure to American movies, I was sure everyone would be wearing Bermuda shorts. I had never seen any in real life, let alone owned a pair. Undeterred, I called the one American girl I knew to explain the situation. "Would you please lend me a pair of Bermuda shorts?" I pleaded. "I really want to fit in." She took pity on me.

Gathering with the others on the first day of our climb, I proudly appeared in my thoroughly American outfit, certain I would look like everyone else. To my embarrassment, no one else wore shorts—of any description. The men dressed in long pants, and the only other woman in the party wore culottes—another strange fashion I'd never seen before. My green plaid Bermudas couldn't be ignored, but Jim's friends were kind. None of them laughed.

Before long, Jim shouted, "Let's go!" and off went the Smith expedition to conquer Mt. Kilimanjaro. Clutching a walking stick in one hand and suntan lotion in the other, I trudged along, doing my best to keep up with the group. Sweating our way through dense banana plantations, we eventually broke free of the vegetation, emerging at the beginning of the trail. The path leading upward toward the summit lay before us. Our adventure had begun.

We arrived at the first overnight hut late in the day. Tired and desperately thirsty, we stumbled inside the hut to find a scene straight out of a Hemingway novel. A white linen tablecloth covered a table, and laid on it, in very proper British style, were china cups filled with steaming hot tea and plates piled high with bread and cake. Afternoon tea was being served by porters trained in British-style mountain climbing. I had to chuckle at the look of utter disbelief on everyone's face.

Two days later, at 15,000 feet, and with snow falling softly, we reached the third and final overnight hut. Shivering, everyone snuggled in sleeping bags, awaiting the 2 a.m. call to begin climbing the frozen gravel leading to the summit. Everyone except me, that is. With a pounding headache and nausea, it quickly became obvious that I couldn't tolerate the altitude. I didn't dare go any higher.

At first light, one of the guides led me down the mountain to wait for the others at the second hut. For an adventure-challenged female, I didn't think I'd done too badly.

As for the rest rooms, there were three—one outside each overnight hut. They sloped backward, the doors wouldn't shut, and, of course, the toilets didn't flush.

An Appetite for Adventure

Today, adventure calls men and women of every age. College students traipse around Europe. Aging baby boomers and retirees videotape their way through Asia. Singles and young marrieds cycle across deserts or hurtle down raging rivers, craving the thrill of living on the edge. Whatever season of life we're in, whatever dangers we face, our appetite for adventure seems insatiable.

Enticed by television shows, "must go" prices for all-in-one vacation packages, and brochures featuring people exactly like us lurching on camels past the pyramids or jumping off platforms tied to giant rubber bands, we eagerly sign up and pay up. Poling down a jungle river on a bamboo raft makes the annual two-week vacation by a local lake look pretty tame. Surely, the advertisements seem to imply, every red-blooded adventurer needs thrills, spills, and huge bills to prove they are alive.

Now, in case you think I'm a thrill-seeker, let me assure you that I am not in the least bit adventuresome when it comes to anything involving physical discomfort or danger. Although I'll always treasure the thrills and chills of climbing Kilimanjaro, challenge me to climb a rock wall, cross a swinging bridge, or fly in a mosquito-sized plane, and I'll have no problem declaring, "Not unless my life depends on it."

I wear my "Wimpy Woman" badge with honor, even if it means being looked down upon by more daring members of the human race.

Yet, I do want my life to be an adventure—a remarkable experience. Don't you? After all, would you willingly choose a ho-hum existence over exploring the unknown, experiencing the unexpected, stretching your limits, and growing into someone you never were before? I don't believe many people would—because God has made us to hunger for more than mere existence.

But—can life really be an adventure unless we leave home and head off to more exotic places? Is it possible for wimps whose courage level hovers around zero? And let's be realistic about the cost. Sometimes our budgets won't stretch to fly the family to Grandma's house, let alone halfway around the world. Must we, then, give up all hope of adventure, believing it's limited to the bold and brave or the financially blessed?

It's easy to think that, isn't it?

My Life, an Adventure?

Do most of your days seem a rerun of the day before? Are you often tempted to think boredom is your destiny? Ever found yourself brooding:

- Susie's life sparkles with adventure, but mine sure doesn't. How come she gets to zip through life in the fast lane while I sit here going nowhere?

- How could my life be an adventure? I'm isolated at home changing diapers ten times a day and wiping cereal off the walls before it hardens like cement. I struggle not to look like something the cat dragged in when my husband walks through the door—not that it makes much difference. Some adventure. Ha.

- Okay, so I know God and try to walk with Him, but how can my life be called an adventure? I go to work day in and day out. Fight traffic. Stare at a computer screen for eight hours. Try to avoid hassles with people around me. Then go home and stare at the tube until bedtime. Some adventure.

You might not identify with these scenarios, but change the details and maybe you'd also chime in, "My life, an adventure? I don't think so."

Let's be honest. If we look at our lives *only from a human perspective*, they can seem pretty routine much of the time. After all, what's so exciting about nursing one sick child after another, tackling never-ending projects, or sitting in traffic jams day after day? Life *can* feel like one long round of dull, daily duties—a treadmill we can't escape from. What's more, if we define adventure as constant thrills, nonstop exhilaration, warm fuzzies, and ideal circumstances, most of us are going to be disappointed.

Limiting your dream of adventure to exploring the exotic or risking life and limb is an easy mistake to make. Just because you haven't tasted too many thrills or traveled far from home doesn't mean your life is insignificant and unimportant. Believe this lie and you'll miss the truth Scripture so clearly reveals:

God has a unique adventure planned for you.

Sprinkled through each chapter in this book are opportunities for you to stop and jot down responses, thoughts, or prayers. This is to help you take the time to process what you're reading and to hear what God is saying to you. For the same reason, at the back of this book you'll find study questions for each chapter. Use these to help you dig deeper, either on your own or with a small group. As you read, give yourself a gift of great value: the time to pause, ponder, and pray.

Get to know yourself more fully by reflecting on what you've read, then jot down your responses to the following.

• What spells *adventure* to you?

• Recall the greatest adventure you've experienced. What makes it stand out?

- As you think about your life, how do you feel about where you are today? Would you say you view life as an adventure? Why, or why not?

Adventure Begins With God

Two thousand years before Jesus was born, God had a unique adventure in mind for one particular man.[1] Appearing to Abraham, He said, "I want you to go on a trip with me. Accept my invitation, and we'll have a great experience together" (Acts 7:2-3, my paraphrase).

Now imagine if you were drifting off to sleep one night, and God said something similar to you: *"Hey, I want you to get up and go to Timbuktu. I've got a unique adventure planned just for you."* What would you say? Would you choose to risk and move into the unknown—or would you dig in your heels, refusing to move out of your comfort zone?

Abraham had no idea where following God would take him. Nor was he given a detailed picture of what God had in mind for his life. Yet in spite of knowing so little, he moved forward in response to God's call. Without so much as a road map, motel reservations, or information from the local tourist bureau, Abraham set off. Step by step he began a journey that was to last his whole life as he walked with God toward a more glorious future than he'd ever dreamed possible.

Abraham's life vividly demonstrates what it means to grow in faith. And that's what we want to discover in this book—those daily choices that draw us closer to God and invite Him to use our lives.

Abraham models what the seeking heart yearns for—to trust God, love Him, and bring Him joy. Because of his faith and devotion, his name is mentioned throughout the Bible. Known as "God's friend" and "the father of all who believe," Abraham strides across history, revered by Christian, Jew, and Muslim alike (James 2:23; Rom. 4:11). As a result of one man's faith, the nation of Israel came to exist, the Scriptures were written, and Jesus Christ came into the world through Mary. What an example.

Abraham wasn't perfect, however. He experienced failure, just as we do. Yet in trying to figure out what it means to walk with the God of history at the beginning of a new millennium, there's no better model for us to learn from.

As you move through each chapter looking at Abraham's strengths and weaknesses, you'll discover important principles for your own walk with God. What are some of these? The importance of saying yes when God speaks, daring to put faith into action, handling conflict God's way, and many more.

Now, in case you're protesting, "But just a minute. Abraham was merely a man who lived thousands of years ago in a vastly different environment. What am I supposed to learn from him?" Let me challenge you: Why not find out?

In God's wisdom, you and I can learn from other people, both men and women, whether they lived in the ancient past or are alive today. Don't close your mind and heart to what God wants you to hear. Instead, be open to His voice and act on what He says.

I don't know where following God will take me. Neither did Abraham. Neither do you. Even so, we can be assured by Scripture that the same God who called and led Abraham, and countless others who responded to Him, will guide and lead us through the adventure called "life."

"I the Lord do not change" (Mal. 3:6). Therefore: "[Most] blessed is the man (or woman) who believes in, trusts in *and* relies on the Lord, and whose hope *and* confidence the Lord is" (Jer. 17:7 Amplified Bible, parentheses author's).

Develop a Seeking Heart

When we come to Jesus, He begins to mold and develop our faith because we're important to Him. Getting saved is step one—the beginning of our adventure. But new birth isn't the be-all and end-all, the sum and substance of the Christian life—there's more.

God's goal is to move each of us from being spiritual babies to mature believers, just as He did with Abraham. This is the ongoing part of our spiritual adventure. Stagnating in spiritual infancy is never His intention. He wants us to cultivate a seeking heart and move forward.

Maybe you began your walk with God having no idea what it meant to live as a Christian. I certainly didn't know about the Holy Spirit and His power to change me. And I didn't have a clue how to handle my temper or my tongue. Fortunately for us, He's patient, sees our heart, and encourages us to keep walking toward maturity.

The writer of Hebrews exhorts: "Let us ... go on to maturity" (Heb. 6:1). Paul's goal also went beyond seeing people come to faith in Christ. He yearned to "present everyone perfect in Christ" (Col. 1:28). What does this mean? That we can somehow become perfect, without messed-up motives, nasty thoughts, or grumpy attitudes ever again? I wish.

Perfection is not going to happen in this life, but the opportunity to become more Christlike happens every day. Think of those times when you're irritated, disappointed, hurt, or mad at someone's unfair treatment of you. Aren't these all opportunities to grow? What about waiting for God to act or for a difficult child to shape up—aren't these times to spiritually stretch and develop a deeper faith or greater self-control? Every situation that is less than perfect can be a spiritual adventure—an opportunity to move forward with God.

Developing spiritual maturity is an exciting process. Beginning at your spiritual birth and continuing throughout your life, let growth be an ongoing goal, a magnet that draws you toward God.

Remember, no one changes instantly, nor does time by itself produce Christlike character. Spiritual growth requires regular intake of the Word, both the Old and New Testaments. Maturity demands prayer that goes beyond "God bless me and my family" as we race out the door to work, school, or into the world. Sharing our faith, serving others, and spending time with those who are growing themselves are other dynamic ingredients that produce change.

Speaking of God's lifelong work in us, J. Oswald Sanders, author and missionary statesman, says, "When God is developing a life for eternity, He is in no hurry. A pumpkin will mature in three months, but an oak tree takes a century, and there are no shortcuts. This principle of growth is equally applicable in the spiritual realm."[2]

God isn't in the pumpkin business. He wants to produce oaks.

Growth God's Way

Can we know what growth is? Are there ways maturity can be seen? Can we know what God wants us to pray for, not only for others but also for ourselves? Inspired by the Holy Spirit, Paul gives us answers in Colossians 1:9-12:

> We have not stopped praying for you and asking God to fill you with the knowledge of his will through all spiritual wisdom and understanding. And we pray this in order that you may live a life worthy of the Lord and

may please him in every way: bearing fruit in every good work, growing in the knowledge of God, being strengthened with all power according to his glorious might so that you may have great endurance and patience, and joyfully giving thanks to the Father who has qualified you to share in the inheritance of the saints in the kingdom of light.

If you want to figure out how to walk with God, here's a good place to begin. Paul mentions six specific areas of growth:

1. *Knowing God's will through spiritual wisdom and understanding*

2. *Living a life worthy of the Lord, pleasing Him in every way*

3. *Bearing fruit in every good work*

4. *Growing in knowledge of God*

5. *Being strengthened with all power ... so you might have great endurance and patience*

6. *Joyfully giving thanks to the Father*

Whether you're a new believer or have been walking with God a long time, growth is possible. Growing in Christ stimulates your mind and satisfies your heart because God made you for this. Start putting these six areas of growth into practice and you'll open the door to daily adventure. You'll discover you *can* be different, you *can* experience the unexpected, and you *can* stretch yourself beyond previously self-imposed boundaries. Let's see how by peeking into the lives of some fellow travelers.

Spiritual Growth:
The Path to Adventure

1. The Will of God

Learn to know the will of God through spiritual wisdom and understanding.

What's the starting point for walking with God? Learning to know His will. This implies the obvious: God has a will that we can know. If this weren't true, it would be illogical and inconsistent of Him to tell us to know and understand it.

Our primary resource for knowing God's will is through His Word. He gave us the Ten Commandments, not the ten suggestions. He's also clearly revealed His will through principles that cover many of the issues we grapple with on a day-to-day basis. In the next chapter we'll discuss in more detail just how God speaks. For now, let's consider those situations that are neither black nor white, right nor wrong. We need wisdom, but how do we get it?

Cheri's excitement about going on a short-term mission trip with her church was contagious. She wanted to serve God wherever He gave her opportunity, and this trip fulfilled her dreams. However, there was one problem. Steve, her husband, traveled extensively for his job and would be home at the time of the mission trip. "I know Steve wouldn't object to my going," she said. "The problem is, I feel we've been apart way too much this past year. Much as I long to go, I sense God telling me this isn't the right time—our relationship needs priority.

"I prayed a lot for wisdom, and God guided me to Hebrews eleven and the story of Noah, who built an ark to save his family. Noah did something that was costly, and seemed foolish to everyone else, but it was what God told him to do, and he was blessed because he obeyed. Somehow, God alerted Noah to something that hadn't happened yet, something that would endanger his family if he didn't act—and that's what I feel He's done for me. In the end, I felt it wisest not to go."

What principles regarding spiritual wisdom can we learn from Cheri?

- *Expect* the Holy Spirit living in you to guide your mind (John 14:17, 26).

- *Commit* to doing what God shows you—even if it isn't your preference (Ps. 119:112).

- *Ask and trust* God to provide the wisdom and understanding you need (Matt. 7:7-8).

Spiritual wisdom is the discernment God gives to sense His will or direction in a given situation. Often He'll give an insight that opens up a new way of looking at a person or circumstance. This is what happened to Cheri. She sensed God alerting her to an unspoken need in her relationship with Steve. By slowing down long enough to ponder, pray, and be open to God's direction, Cheri felt led to stay home.

"I know I made the right decision for this year," she commented, "but who knows? Maybe Steve and I can go together next time. That would be really exciting."

In addition to clear statements in Scripture about God the Father's will for every believer, He also has a will and plan for each individual life. God knew exactly where Abraham was to go, who was to go with him, and what would happen when he got there. And He knows exactly what He wants to bring about in your life also.

God didn't create you and me, call us to faith in Christ, and then say, "Make your own way in life. It doesn't matter to Me how you live or what you do." Would you say that to your own child? No! Responsible, loving parents help their child discover her strengths, his bent, where that child will be most successful according to how he or she was created. Would God be less concerned and involved than a human parent? Never. Discovering our gifts, abilities, and God's purposes for us is all part of our spiritual adventure.

2. A Life Worthy of the Lord

Live a life worthy of the Lord, pleasing Him in every way.

Have you ever thought, *Just what is my purpose in life?* Here's your answer: God's purpose is for us to please Him in every way— and that's no easy task when we insist on running our own lives.

Two weeks after her marriage to Josh, Marty knew their relationship was in trouble. After a less than idyllic honeymoon, she wondered what the future held. Instead of enjoying "honeymoon years," life became one long struggle to adjust to marriage, motherhood, and other unexpected challenges.

As is true of many couples after they marry, Josh and Marty discovered they didn't know each other very well. Both strong-willed, they clashed over many things, finding little common ground. The emotional strain took its toll. Even though Marty loved the Lord, she wanted to run—to escape from the choices she'd made. Then Marty read David's words in Psalm 139: "Where can I go from your Spirit? Where can I flee from your presence?" (v. 7).

"I groaned at the implications," she said. "No matter where I ran, God would pursue me because He loved me. I knew He had a plan for my life. I was His child, and I knew He'd never let me go, no matter how much I wrestled with Him."

"At the time I read those words," said Marty, "I felt trapped. But as I turned to God in my unhappiness, I learned that submitting my will to Him is essential if I'm ever to live a life worthy of the

Lord. I can't please Him, or love Josh, unless He helps me because I stumble over my flesh that doesn't want to die and my temperament that clashes with Josh.

"As I keep walking with God, though, He's helping me honestly face these issues. Because He loves me, and because I want to grow, He is helping me learn to live in a way that's a credit to Him."

The inner changes God produced in Marty shouldn't surprise us. After all, isn't this what we hope to see from all the work we put into training and disciplining our own children?

3. Bear Fruit in Every Good Work

Jesus made it clear that if you and I abide in Him, we *will* bear fruit. The evidence of His life in us can be as simple as deliberately walking across the room to talk to someone sitting alone at a church social or as involved as taking someone in need into our home. We've been created to do good works. This is what God wants to see in our lives. In fact, knowing our strengths and our circumstances, He prepared these good works in advance for us to carry out (Eph. 2:10).

Has it ever occurred to you that your job is also a "good work" given by God? That He wants it to be a place of spiritual adventure—a place where you bear fruit and show evidence of His presence in you? Don't forget: Your work situation might limit what you can say about your faith, *but it can't stop you from living it out.*

Jami, a labor and delivery nurse, views her work as a place where she can bear the fruit of the Spirit and grow closer to Christ at the same time.

"I have to depend on God to help me be strong and able to handle emotionally difficult situations," she said. "Most of the time a child's delivery is exciting, but when the baby dies, it's hard for the family as well as for me. I cry with them, and all the while I'm praying that God will bring His good through this pain and draw them closer to Him.

"After gently wrapping the baby in a blanket, I encourage the parents to hold their little one for as long as they want. If there are severe deformities, I try to present the baby looking as normal as possible and comment on how beautiful he or she is. Of course, I can't help but wonder what God's doing when such a thing happens. As I take care of each family, though, I ask the Lord to teach me about His power and control even in situations that hurt so badly."

Your job, whether at home or in the workplace, may be less stressful than Jami's, but it, too, contains opportunities to express the love of Jesus. In fact, every day has opportunities if we'll only open our eyes and act on what the Spirit leads us to do. God hasn't called us to an adventure with Him for our sake alone, He wants to encourage, lift up, and give hope to others *through* us. "This is to my Father's glory," said Jesus, "that you bear much fruit, showing yourselves to be my disciples" (John 15:8).

4. Grow in the Knowledge of God

One of the challenges all Christians face in the twenty-first century is to know *what* we believe. You and I must be able to present the biblical view of God in a biblically ignorant world. Was God "a man who became divine," as one fast-growing religion claims? *No!* Are we all God? *No!* Is God "the Oneness found in all created things"? *No!* Paul urged the Christians of his day to grow in the knowledge of God, who He is and what it means to walk with Him. His appeal is just as urgent to our generation.

Growing in your knowledge of God is an essential part of experiencing life as a spiritual adventure. Beginning with a grasp of who He is as revealed in the Bible, move on to knowing God as the One who longs to draw you into a love relationship with himself. He wants you to sense His closeness and feel secure enough to bring Him all your concerns, struggles, and questions. In this kind of relationship you'll get to know His heart and discover you never need to fear His rejection, condemnation, or abandonment. When you come trustingly into His presence, He'll not only teach you about himself, He'll also teach you about yourself.

Natalie loved the speaking ministry God led her into. Although constantly humbled and delighted by the response she received from many women, she struggled with insecurity. Whenever she heard of another speaker's success, feelings of discouragement and worthlessness swept over her.

"I was tired of battling these feelings," she confided, "so I took time out to talk to the Lord about it. I asked Him straight out for insight into the root of my problem. Was I jealous? Envious? Sorry for myself? I despised the thought of having such ugly emotions.

"As I prayed, God showed me what lay behind my discouragement. Deep down, I equated invitations to speak with His acceptance and approval, and the lack of invitations with His disapproval.

"Even though I knew from the Word this wasn't true, I couldn't change how I felt," she continued. "God showed me I needed to question these feelings and counter them with truth from Scripture every time they came back. I'm learning that every time I take my struggles or confusion to Him, I discover more about Him and more about where I need to grow."

5. Grow Strong

Be strengthened with all power according to His glorious might so that you may have great endurance and patience.

Have you ever said in exasperation, "I can't stand waiting?" Or moaned in exhaustion to the Lord, "How much longer will I have to live with this?" What happens when you face frustrating or frightening circumstances in your own strength? Too often the result is either a furious blowup or a tearful breakdown.

Difficult circumstances happen in life—an unexpected illness, job downsizing, marriage or family problems, church dissension. Who wants them? Not me! God doesn't shield us from tough experiences, much as we wish He would, because He knows we grow from them—but only if we turn to Him for help.

"I'm not jealous of my sister," remarked Janet as we talked over coffee, "even though she has six kids and I'm infertile. It's tough, but I'm praying that Jack and I will have children one day—but right now isn't exactly the best time."

Seeing my quizzical look, Janet went on to explain. "The reason I'm not depressed and completely focused on getting pregnant is that I realize our marriage needs work. I know God is able to grow both of us, and He's in control of when and if we have children.

"Interestingly, while Jack and I work at improving our relationship and wait for a baby, I sense God encouraging me to be spiritually fruitful in the lives of other women. I really enjoy discipling younger women and just love being with their kids. Naturally, I wish God would make our struggles go away, but I know He's using them for our good.

"What positives do I see from being infertile and in a difficult marriage? How about: learning to trust His wisdom and timing, having more time to invest in other moms, developing patience, and finding inner strength through prayer to keep loving Jack."

Spiritual maturity develops when we begin to trust that God is *always* at work for our ultimate good, a truth Janet is discovering. Being strengthened supernaturally in a tough time is also a vivid witness to the reality of God and part of our spiritual adventure. The exciting result? Realizing our faith is no longer theory but has moved into the realm of real-life experience, maturing us into someone we never were before.

6. Joyfully Give Thanks to the Father

"Say thank you to Daddy," I instructed our two young children, Malaika and Elliot.

"Thank you, Daddy, for taking us out for pizza," they obediently responded.

Training children to be thankful is part of a parent's job description. Of course, what we really hope is to hear these magic words spontaneously slip out of their mouths, whereupon we beam with pride at the good manners of our little angels. As we wait for that day, however, we doggedly persist in training them to express gratitude whether they feel it (right then) or not.

As our heavenly Father, God looks to see an attitude of gratitude develop in us. Thankfulness shows our awareness of what God has done for you and me. As spiritual babies, we might only look at outward circumstances, and if they're good we'll give thanks. But what happens when life doesn't go well, when we hit some bumps in the road? Does our attitude turn sour and become "Why should I give thanks when God let this happen?"

Christian maturity takes us to a deeper level than being thankful for a new car or a big bonus, or even for a medical test that came back with good results. Of course these make us thankful to God. That's the right response. However, God has done far more awesome deeds on our behalf: "[He] has made us fit to share in all the wonderful things that belong to those who live in the Kingdom of light" (Col. 1:12 The Living Bible). We've been rescued from Satan's power, and Christ has forgiven us, bringing you and me into an eternal relationship with Him. He's given us a new nature that is changing the way you and I look at life and ourselves. No wonder we're to be thankful, and can be thankful, in spite of our earthly circumstances.

Give thanks to the Father; overflow with thankfulness; sing with gratitude in your hearts to God; be watchful and thankful, urges the Spirit (Col. 1:3, 12; 2:7; 3:16; 4:2). God deserves ceaseless thanks for stepping into our lives and never giving up on us. The more we realize who He is and what He has done, the greater our joy and delight. Thankfulness flows when *He*, rather than our fluctuating moods or circumstances, is our focus.

Paul's prayer for the Colossians is Christ's prayer for you and me. He wants us to mature, to show evidence in everyday life that He is at work in us.

- To help you take another step forward, look back at the six areas we've covered and note which one most needs attention.

- Now spend a few moments asking God what He wants you to do to grow in this area. Write down what comes to mind as well as a step you can take, perhaps today.

If you think God called you to a boring, ho-hum existence—lose that thought. He hasn't. Jesus promised you life—eternal life after you die, *and* abundant life now. You can't change the past, or other people, but you can choose to walk with God through whatever happens *today*. Make this your habit and life *will* become a spiritual adventure, even if you never get to leave home.

Daily Choices for the Growing Heart
View Life as an Adventure

- Choose to view every day as a spiritual adventure—an opportunity to experience God.

- Refuse to allow your circumstances, personality, background, age, education, or energy level to become a barrier to seeking God.

- Respond whenever you sense God's presence. Make growing closer to Him your life objective. Let yourself be stretched beyond your self-imposed boundaries.

- Follow His will for you. Risk new experiences, discovering His reality in ways you can't imagine right now.

- Grow in knowledge and thankfulness, watching as God divinely molds you into who He intends you to be.

- Commit yourself to walking with God and eagerly watch for Him to turn your life into an adventure.

Two

When God Speaks, Say "Yes"

Obedience: To Hear and to Act

*M*oving my shoulders rhythmically up and down, and chanting, "Hmm, hmm," I tried my best to imitate the Masaii choir performing on stage. Sitting in the back row of the Brackenhurst Conference Center's auditorium, a few miles outside Nairobi, I laughed as the man in the next seat looked quizzically at me. *Who knows,* I thought mischievously, *maybe somewhere way back I have African blood!*

Twenty years after leaving Kenya, Jim and I had been invited back to participate in a conference for missionary doctors and their spouses. The smell of woodsmoke, the sound of women chattering in the surrounding tea plantations, and the smart salute of the guard at the gate brought back warm memories.

Seated in the packed auditorium, God imprinted another memory on my heart—the thrilling sight and sound of young Masaii men and women praising God in their own language and style. Singing Scripture put to tribal tunes, they stamped their feet, moved their shoulders up and down, and occasionally whooped and jumped high in the air, making the room come alive with joy. African blood or not, I couldn't help joining in.

Nor could I help thinking back to those early unknown missionaries to the Masaii. *Could they have had any idea of the impact of their lives? Did they, by faith, believe the day would come when there would be Masaii churches, pastors, and choirs?* Tears crept down my cheeks as I thought of the difficulties they willingly faced to bring the good news of Jesus Christ to this proud, nomadic tribe.

That unique experience of listening to a Masaii choir often flashes in my mind. But stop for a minute and think about what happened to make that choir a reality. What lies behind the fact that people from every nation, not only the Masaii, now celebrate God's love in Christ? The answer is simple yet profound. Ordinary men and women said yes when God broke into their lives, inviting them to walk with Him. Their response, like Abraham's, had far greater implications than they ever could have dreamed.

What's So Important About Saying Yes?

Choosing to obey God is not always easy. Our human tendency is to want to call the shots, to decide what we want to do. We also think we know the best path to take and can figure out how to handle our problems. God knows this, having watched human beings going their own way from the beginning. Author Wayne Detzler says, "In this day of self-indulgence, the entire concept of obedience appears to be out of date, but it is the secret of spiritual living."[1] No matter how difficult yielding your will might be at times, saying yes is essential if you want to move forward with God.

Let's look at some reasons why.

- **God Is the Creator of All.**

"The Lord is the everlasting God, the Creator of the ends of the earth" (Isa. 40:28). God has a right to your obedience because of who He is: Eternally Existent, Almighty, All-Knowing, totally Holy, Just, and Loving. He created you for fellowship with himself and calls you to respond to His love by walking in obedience.

- **God Is Your Maker.**

"When I was woven together in the depths of the earth, your eyes saw my unformed body. All the days ordained for me were written in your book before one of them came to be" (Ps. 139:15-16).

God understands how you're formed and how you tick. Being all-wise, He knows what's best for you better than you do. He doesn't command obedience out of a perverse desire to deny you joy or fulfillment, but because He knows the damage that comes from going along certain paths. His commands are given for your protection. If you're wise, you'll follow what He says.

- **Jesus Is Your Savior.**

Jesus died to give you God's best: freedom from a guilty conscience and power to live a productive and positive life. He washes away all the junk that has gone on in your life. You no longer need to fear standing before God, because Jesus died to pay the penalty for your sin. Through the Holy Spirit, Jesus promises inner peace, healing from life's hurts and wounds, and power over your tendencies to hurt others and yourself. In addition, He fills your human need for purpose, significance, and security. In light of the price Christ paid to bring you into a relationship with God the Father, you're called to live in obedience: "Do not let sin reign in your mortal body so that you obey its evil desires ... but rather offer yourselves to God" (Rom. 6:12-13).

- **Jesus Loves You Unconditionally.**

The extent of Jesus' love can't be doubted when you consider the Cross. He, in turn, calls you to show your love by doing what He

31

asks (John 14:21). Obedience proves you mean what you claim: that you belong to Jesus Christ, He is Lord of your life, and you love and trust Him. When you choose obedience, not only does God see but so do others. Disobedience doesn't cut you off from His eternal love, but it does hinder your fellowship with Him, block His blessing, and cause others to stumble. Because He loves you, what He asks you to do is always for your eternal best. Obedience shows you believe this.

The root word for obedience means "to hear." God doesn't tell us merely to hear what He says and decide for ourselves how to respond. He commands us to obey. "Do not merely listen to the word, and so deceive yourselves. Do what it says" (James 1:22). Long before James challenged Christians to do what God says, Abraham did just that. He went forward in obedience, experiencing, step by step, a relationship with God that far exceeded any earthly dreams of adventure or success.

Does God want your life journey and mine to be an adventure? Absolutely. In fact, He urges us to "taste and see that the Lord is good." And obedience is the key.

God Takes the Initiative

How much Abraham first knew about God is a mystery. Even if his knowledge was meager, however, his life vividly illustrates the attitude that underpins all spiritual progress: Abraham chose to say yes when God spoke to him.

In recounting Israel's history, Stephen said, "The God of glory appeared to our father Abraham while he was still in Mesopotamia, before he lived in Haran. 'Leave your country and your people,' God said, 'and go to the land I will show you.' So he left" (Acts 7:2-4). Can you imagine responding like that?

Here was Abraham—already well into mid-life—firmly settled in Ur, a thriving city deep in ancient Iraq. He didn't live in some boring backwater. Ur was famous for worship of the moon god, its schools, libraries, and businesses, as well as its hanging gardens.

Visiting London's British Museum many years ago, I looked with awe at the pottery, jewelry, and other artifacts archeologists had dug up in Ur. The thought of God appearing to a real man, in a real place, at a specific time in history thrilled me. Abraham's story is not a myth. God broke into his life, calling him to move forward, to walk with Him into a new land.

Does it excite you to realize that this same God also calls *you* to follow Him, step by step, into His purposes for you?

To help you say yes to His plans, God wants you to know:

- He sought you out.
- He loves you unconditionally.
- He speaks to you.
- He leads you forward as you walk in obedience.

Sought by God

From Genesis to Revelation, the Bible shouts the message, "God knows and cares about you!" Far from being a distant deity with no concern for His creation, Scripture shows us a God who breaks into human lives. He doesn't sit around in heaven waiting for us to desire Him; He takes the initiative.

Paul affirms this in his astounding statement that those who come to Christ were chosen in Him before the foundation of the world (Eph. 1:4). Like an eager lover, God takes the first step, making us aware of His love and drawing us to respond. The apostle John adds, "This is love: not that we loved God, but that he loved us and sent his Son as an atoning sacrifice for our sins" (1 John 4:10). God purposefully seeks us out. Nothing can block His plan.

"Is Anything Too Hard for the Lord?"

Drafted into Hitler's army near the end of World War II, Jurgen Moltmann was sent to fight Allied troops invading Europe. Poorly trained and equipped, he and hundreds of other young men were thrown into battle. A short time later he literally stumbled into a trench filled with British soldiers.

Taken to a prisoner-of-war camp in Belgium, he and other young German soldiers heard for the first time of the horrors committed by their nation against the Jews. Many fell into severe depression. Sickened and ashamed, some gave up the will to live.

In the camp, Jurgen Moltmann received a New Testament from the chaplain and read for the first time of God's love and forgiveness. "I found God," he said. "Or rather, God found me."

Sent to Scotland at the end of the war, he worked with other prisoners repairing the damage done by Hitler's bombs. While there, Christians befriended him and helped him grow in Christ. Today, Jurgen Moltmann is an influential theologian.

You might think, *I found God*, but the astounding truth is, God found you. Before you were even aware of God, He was aware of you. God knows the exact circumstances to use to break into your life— perhaps an unhappy marriage, a divorce, loneliness or emptiness, a hunger for more joy or purpose, the aching need to find forgiveness. Whatever the circumstances that draw you to Him, God takes the initiative and seeks you out. If you've put your faith in Jesus Christ, you can say with Jurgen Moltmann, "God found me."

- Take a moment to think about this. What was happening in your life when God found you? What did you feel as a result? Did God clearly direct your early steps in some way? Write down what comes to mind and give Him praise.

Loved Unconditionally

Have you ever wondered why God bothered to break into your life? Or why He cares about you? King David wondered about these same things. He asked God, "What is man that you are mindful of him, the son of man that you care for him?" (Ps. 8:4). The answer has nothing to do with who we are. God loves us because of who He is: God is love.

Think about someone you love, or have loved deeply. Whether this was an adult or child, what did you yearn for? Didn't you want to be with that person, to express your love, to share your experiences, to enjoy his or her company? The relationship God wants with you and me is no different.

If your mind was imprinted with the idea that love and acceptance depended on your grades in school, your weight, or making the cheerleading squad, it will seem unbelievable that God accepts and loves you unconditionally. This concept is hard for us to believe, because the world we live in doesn't operate like that—but *God does*.

God knows that to fully accomplish His purposes in your life, you need a strong sense of His unconditional love. If you feel God can't or won't love you because of some failure in your life, you put yourself on an emotional roller coaster.

As a giggly adolescent, did you ever pick petals off a daisy one at a time, chanting, "He loves me, he loves me not"? I did—many times! We can play that game in regard to how God feels toward us. For instance, say you've told a big lie to get out of an awkward situation, and now you wonder, *Does He love me, or doesn't He?* If you're unsure of God's acceptance, and mistakenly think it's based on how good you are rather than the righteousness of Christ, you're going to struggle emotionally.

Say Yes to God's Love

One of God's greatest gifts is the assurance of His love, based not on what we do, but on what Christ did on the cross. "Righteousness from God comes through faith in Jesus Christ to all who believe.... We have been justified through faith.... There is now no condemnation for those who are in Christ Jesus" (Rom. 3:22; 5:1; 8:1). Grasping these amazing truths produces emotional and spiritual stability—and the willingness to trust God when He calls us to act.

Let's be honest—it isn't always easy to do what God asks: forgive someone who's harmed you, release a grudge, stand up for what is right. Believing that God loves you, and only asks for what is pleasing to Him and best for you, is essential. This requires trust. If your earthly parent or another authority figure betrayed you, it's tempting to believe no one can be trusted, not even God. However, God can never be compared to a fallible and sinful person. He is totally pure, loving, and trustworthy—something that cannot be said about any human being.

When God asks you to say yes to something, He points to His character as the basis on which you can trust Him. "The Lord is compassionate and gracious, slow to anger, abounding in love" (Ps. 103:8). His loving-kindness is new, fresh, and at work for you every day. God doesn't ask you to entrust your life to someone you suspect may not have your best interest at heart. He asks you to walk along paths He's prepared for your good. Not alone, but with Him.

Knowing our struggle to believe that an invisible yet all-powerful God could really love and care for us, God impelled the writers of Scripture to make positive declarations of His love and commitment.

To settle in your mind that God can be trusted with your life decisions, take time to look up the following verses. Put your name in the blank spaces and soak your soul in these truths.

- God loves _____ with an everlasting love *today* (John 3:16; Ps. 100:5).

- God has plans to bless _____ *today* (Jer. 29:11).

- God provides all _____ needs to walk with Him *today* (2 Pet. 1:3).

- God calls _____ to follow Him *today* (Mark 1:17).

- God chose _____ to be His and bear fruit *today* (John 15:16).

- Now ask yourself, "Do I believe these statements? Do they make my heart sing? Or are they merely wishful thinking at this point in my life?" Share your honest reactions with God, and then ask Him to fill you with a sense of His love and personal interest in you.

Tasting the reality of these truths, and many others embedded in Scripture, takes more than just knowing about them. They need to be internalized, chewed on, and rehearsed in your mind until you have reprogrammed your habitual thought patterns. This is the process Paul refers to in Romans 12:2: "Do not conform any longer to the pattern of this world [this means the way you think], but be transformed by the renewing of your mind."

Believing with your heart that God loves you deeply, wants your best, and will supply all you need frees you to trust—to say yes to what He asks. Do this and you'll move forward into His purposes for your life.

God, Are You Speaking to Me?

Have you ever wondered how Abraham heard God? Or how you're supposed to hear Him speaking to you? The Bible doesn't state exactly how the God of glory appeared to Abraham. Perhaps He spoke in a vision or a dream. Maybe He appeared in human form, as some believe happened when Jacob wrestled with a man (Gen. 32:24-30). Did Abraham encounter God in some tangible object, as Moses did with the burning bush? We don't know.

Whatever method God used, it's clear Abraham knew this was not indigestion, a fantasy, or wishful thinking. After all, who would get up and leave all they had ever known because they over-indulged the night before?

We might not know how Abraham heard God speak, but Scripture is clear that He communicated with people in the past. God spoke to Adam and Eve in the Garden. He told Moses His plan to free the Israelites, and then directed him for forty years. He gave His message to the prophets, who declared, "The word of the Lord came to me." He spoke during Christ's ministry, and through His life and words. He spoke through the Holy Spirit to men and women in the early church. Knowing this, is there any reason a God who is the same yesterday, today, and forever would stop communicating with us?

The question you and I need to ask ourselves is not "Does God speak today?" but "How do I hear His voice?"

How Do I Hear God's Voice?

Pam and her husband, John, faced a difficult decision and couldn't agree on what to do. To go John's way filled Pam with dread. She wanted to please him, but she knew she would find John's solution extremely stressful and feared it might damage their relationship.

Sharing her struggle, Pam said, "I went for a walk, praying and crying out to God to help me be able to accept this situation if there was no alternative. Breaking into my misery, the Holy Spirit reminded me of several things.

"First, He impressed on me that I was imagining something that had not happened and might never happen. Then He reminded me of Philippians 4:8, that I was to think only about whatever is true, what is real and actual, and not let my imagination run away with me. The third thing He reminded me of is that when I'm afraid, I need to trust Him. I was letting my mind be overwhelmed with the Enemy's whispers of *How will you cope?* and lots of other scary thoughts."

Pam needed to hear from God. She hadn't known what to do, so she was falling to pieces emotionally. Using His Word, God guided her mind to think about biblical principles that applied to her situation:

- Keep your mind focused on what is true, not imaginary.
- Trust God to lead your life.
- Don't worry, because worry can't change your situation; only God can.

After hearing God speak through His Word, Pam faced a choice—to trust God, or apply all the pressure she could on John.

"I made a deliberate decision that night not to worry," Pam said. "Whenever I found myself thinking about what might happen, I reminded myself that I was trusting God to sort it out. I also realized that it might never happen, but if it did, God would give me the strength to go through it at that time, not before."

Hard as it was for John to let go of what he wanted to do, he recognized Pam's great distress, and ultimately chose to let the matter drop. Looking back, Pam gratefully acknowledged what God did. "He spoke clearly to me that night," she recalled. "He helped me choose to trust Him and not to fear. Then, some time after I'd taken that step, He touched John's heart."

By saying yes to God's voice, Pam's panic turned into peace. "I took a major step forward that night," she said. "I learned that listening to God and doing what He says in the Word really does work."

God Speaks Through:

His Word

How did God speak to Pam? Taking her knowledge of His Word, He brought relevant passages to mind. She might not have been able to quote them word for word, but she understood the principles that applied to her situation.

God's primary means of communicating His will comes through the Bible. Not knowing what it says hinders our ability to hear Him speak. Whether you're a baby Christian or have been a believer for some time, regular reading and studying of Scripture is essential for knowing what God wants you to do in a given situation. But beware the danger of taking verses out of context.

An old joke describes a Christian trying to discern God's will. Opening the Bible at random, he read, "Judas hanged himself." Looking for more insight, he turned the next few pages. This time he read, "Go and do likewise." Frantic, he turned to yet another passage, which said, "And what you do, do quickly." This is not what God means when He says His Word is a lamp to our feet and a light for our path.

Listening in Prayer

Prayer isn't meant to be a monologue. Solomon wrote, "There's a time to be silent, and a time to speak" (Eccles. 3:7). This is as true in our relationship with God as it is with any other person. You don't have to chant a mantra, burn incense, or twist your legs like a pretzel to hear from God. Just sit quietly before Him.

Listen also for God's voice when you're praying. As you bring a job or family problem to Him, be alert to a possible solution that hasn't yet occurred to you. When praying for wisdom, listen for His leading—is it to share your concern with someone who can give you spiritual insight? Is it to seek out a book or other resource that might help?

Being silent and listening doesn't come naturally to most of us, but that's the way to hear what's on someone's heart. It's no different with God.

His Spirit

This is God speaking to us from within. For instance, as you're reading the Word, His inner voice applies what you're reading to your particular situation. You can sense the Spirit saying, "Pay attention. Stop and look at that verse again."

He also speaks at unexpected moments. Driving my children to school several years ago, the thought kept repeating, *Go and visit Eva*. This seemed a ridiculous idea. After all, I reasoned, who goes and visits someone at 8:30 in the morning? But the idea wouldn't go away. On my way home I decided to stop by her house, not knowing what I was going to say.

Eva opened the door, eyes red and puffy, and clutching a tissue. "I felt I should come," was all I could say before Eva spoke. "I've been on my knees for the last hour crying to the Lord for someone to help me."

In our fear of being thought fanatical or strange, we can easily miss the gentle leading of the Holy Spirit and His desire to use us. Don't ignore His promptings to pray for someone who comes to mind, to make a phone call, to speak to a person He points out as looking depressed, lonely, or confused. Listen for His voice as He speaks to your spirit and follow what He says. If you find your concern had no basis, then just thank the Lord for giving you a tender heart. There's no need to be embarrassed about showing God's love to others. Keep responding whenever you sense the Spirit speaking.

Let me give you a word of caution, however. Many people claim "God told me to   " (fill in the blank), yet what they did clearly bears no resemblance to what Jesus would do. There is a plumb line against which you and I need to measure what we think God is saying: The Holy Spirit will always guide us into truth, not error or evil. What He leads you to do will always be consistent with Scripture. If an inner voice tells you to do anything that contradicts God's Word or character, *it is not from Him.*

Mature Christians

Proverbs 18:15 says, "The heart of the discerning acquires knowledge; the ears of the wise seek it out." When your spiritual antenna is up and you're eager to hear God's voice, He speaks. Listen carefully to your pastor or Bible study leader, to a godly relative, older believer, or to a spiritually alive friend who shares a verse with you. These are all ways God might speak.

Seek out those who encourage you to live fully for the Lord and ask for their input. When you're reading a Christian book or magazine, or listening to a Christian radio or television program, keep alert. When you hear Him, whether whispering or shouting, be like Samuel, who said, "Speak, Lord, for your servant is listening" (1 Sam. 3:9).

Your Conscience

Does God speak through your conscience? Yes, if it is programmed by His Word and not the world around you. The more data you put into your heart and mind regarding God's moral and ethical standards, the more reliable your conscience. Remember, God's Word is the plumb line.

Terri bought a new computer, but it came without any of her favorite software. In response to her moaning about the extra cost involved in buying the software, her adult son, Alan, said, "Hey, Mom, no problem. Just borrow mine." Wanting time to consider what she should do, Terri responded, "Well, let me think about it." She knew that installing someone else's software was illegal—but she didn't want to spend the extra money to buy her own.

"In the end my conscience wouldn't let me take up Alan's offer," said Terri. "I'd tried to raise him to follow the Lord, so how could I now agree to do something illegal just because I wanted to save money?"

Hoping Alan wouldn't think her a religious crackpot, she explained her reasoning to him. "I understand," he said to Terri's relief and delight.

By acting with integrity, you'll not only enjoy inner peace, you might also have the opportunity to show others that your heart is set on following God. Let your conscience be your guide—as long as your conscience is guided by God.

Circumstances

Trying to hear God's voice through circumstances can be a little like reading tea leaves. It all depends on how you interpret what you hear. Difficult circumstances do not necessarily indicate you are out of God's will. Nor do good times prove all is spiritually well, either. Many other factors need to be considered.

When trying to discern God's voice through circumstances, stop and ask yourself some questions:

- Do I have a sense of hope and feel God's encouragement to go this way—or am I struggling with doubt and feelings of hopelessness?

- Does the Word give me freedom to move in this direction?

- Have I prayed and listened for the Spirit's voice?

- Have I talked to mature believers and asked for impartial advice?

- Do I have peace in my conscience?

When the answer is yes to each of these questions, you can be confident God is speaking.

Obedience—The Key to Moving Forward

Imagine the scene. The morning after God appeared to him, Abraham rushed into his father's room to say he had to move. No, he didn't know where. No, he didn't have a detailed plan. He just had to move. I wonder what kind of response he got—especially when he tried to convince Sarah that camping would be lots of fun.

What God asked Abraham to do would be equivalent to you or me living in New York and being called by God to trek across an unexplored North America to settle on the unknown West Coast. Abraham's conviction that God had spoken to him and he must obey was unshakable. God had said leave your country and your people. Abraham was prepared to do this, but God had also said, leave your father's household. This he failed to do.

Loading up the family camels and donkeys, Abraham and his father, Terah, his nephew Lot, and his wife, Sarah, set out. After traveling hundreds of miles in hot, dusty conditions, they arrived in Haran and decided to enjoy a little rest and relaxation. Not surprisingly, the appeal of continuing their journey across hundreds of miles of desert gradually waned. Haran was the equivalent of grinding to a halt in Chicago. Instead of being a halfway place to recuperate and replenish their supplies, Haran became a place of halfway obedience.

Settling Down Halfway

By settling in Haran, Abraham stopped short of God's purposes for him. Perhaps his father influenced him or there was some other reason. Whatever the cause, it's believed Abraham remained in Haran for possibly five to fifteen years. Nothing is recorded of God's working in his life during this time.

Abraham had made a start, filled with faith and confidence, but he got sidetracked from God's call on his life. Sound familiar?

Halfway obedience, partial obedience, incomplete obedience—whatever we call it, hinders God's desire to fully work out His purposes in our lives. Abraham was told clearly to leave his father's household, but he didn't—he took Dad and his nephew Lot with him.

God never asks us to do something without a good reason. He knew Abraham's father, Terah, would hinder His purposes for Abraham. And that's what happened. Abraham allowed his father's influence to keep him from full obedience. It was only after Terah died that Abraham responded once again to God's call (Gen. 11:32-12:4).

Denise understands the power of family. Raised in a chaotic home where drinking, drugs, and casual sex were common, she yearned to find a different way to live. After meeting Chris, a fun-loving young

Christian, she began going to church with him and his family. Denise soon responded to the Gospel, and a few months later she and Chris were married. Wanting to begin a new life together, they moved to another state. Then Denise began to struggle with homesickness.

Talking with Denise after a retreat where I'd been teaching on Abraham, she commented, "When you mentioned that God had a reason for telling Abraham to leave his father's household, I felt He was talking to me. I've been telling Chris that I want to go back home, but I know my family would be a very negative influence. They don't like my being a Christian, and they'd try to keep me from moving forward. I realize, now, God doesn't want us to go back. I can't wait to tell Chris."

Causes and Consequences

Because Abraham didn't obey fully, God didn't move in his life during his stay in Haran. By settling far short of His command, Abraham failed to experience the blessings God had for him at that time. The same is true for us. Whatever the reason for our halfway obedience, we can lull ourselves into thinking all is well between God and us. What we often don't realize is how much spiritual intimacy and power we're missing by closing our ears to His voice. This was Paula's experience.

"I've felt convicted for many years about the importance of memorizing Scripture," confided Paula. "Even though I write verses out on cards and try to follow through, I forget to take them with me in the car or don't get around to sticking them up where I can see them. Now I'm realizing how my bad habits have robbed me of the ability to witness, using God's Word. I also realize how much spiritual insight I've lost out on simply because I never took God's voice seriously enough."

Halfway obedience is not limited to halfhearted Christians. We may all practice it at times. We'll walk with God to a certain degree, but then we sense the Spirit talking to us about disciplining our time—cutting back on the hours spent chatting on the phone or watching television. Perhaps He makes us aware of our tendency to grumble or spend more than we have. Maybe He points out a grudge we're carrying or some other attitude that isn't pleasing to Him. We're conscious God is bringing these things to our attention, but it takes too much effort to deal with them. Like Paula, we want to respond in the right manner, but ...

God says obedience is better than sacrifice for a powerful reason (1 Sam. 15:22). Doing what He says shows we love Him above ourselves and view Him as the only One worthy of our lifelong devotion. We honor Him when we're sensitive to His voice and quick to deal with what He points out. He, in turn, honors those who honor Him.

Pursued by Love

After Terah died, it seems God appeared once again to Abraham and urged him forward (Gen. 12:1). God's love didn't shrivel up and go away because Abraham got sidetracked in Haran. Nor did He scrap His purposes for Abraham's life. What an encouragement to know that God doesn't throw out His plans for us even when we continue in habit patterns or attitudes of halfway obedience. He still speaks. He still pursues.

Once, on a visit to see my parents in England, I watched a sheepdog competition on television. Under the direction of its shepherd, the dog had to herd a flock of sheep from one field to another through a narrow gate. Using a whistle, plus other sounds and gestures, the shepherd directed the sheepdog.

Unfortunately, sheep don't always go in the same direction. Just like human beings, there's always one or more dashing off here or there, trying to go its own way. In response, the dog ran over and blocked, nudged, or cornered the stubborn sheep, making it move along with the flock in the direction the shepherd wanted them to go.

Those sheepdogs reminded me of the Holy Spirit, who pursues us even when we refuse to go along God's path. He comes into our lives when we are stuck in our "Harans," our personal places of halfway obedience, determined to block us from moving further away from Him. Or, He nudges our conscience. Sometimes He gets us in a corner, grabbing our attention through a song, a message, or something we read. Regardless of how long it takes or what methods He employs to draw us back into His paths, God perseveres.

Affirming God's faithfulness, Paul stated, "He who began a good work in you will carry it on to completion until the day of Christ Jesus" (Phil. 1:6). This was true for Abraham, and it is true for you and me.

In response to God's call to move out of Ur, Abraham left all that was familiar. Now God called him once again—this time to leave halfway Haran. His plans for Abraham, and the world through him, lay ahead in the place of full obedience. By making a fresh commitment to follow God's call, Abraham moved into God's eternal plan for mankind. He also said a resounding yes to all the undreamed-of blessings God had in store for him.

What is God waiting to bless your life with once you say yes to Him?

Daily Choices for the Growing Heart
When God Speaks, Say "Yes"

God had undreamed-of blessings in store for Abraham, and He has many blessings in store for you, too. For Abraham to receive what God wanted to give him, however, he had to make choices. The same is true for you and me. Even if you've gone your own way and grown spiritually cold, your choices today can launch you on a new path. Be encouraged by these three truths:

- Recognize that if God is pointing out some place of halfhearted obedience, it's because He loves you and longs for you not to settle for less than His best.

- Rejoice that God doesn't leave you in your "Haran." He wants you out of there and moving forward with Him.

- Respond to the nudging of the Spirit. Abraham knew he had been called for a great purpose, but he allowed his eagerness to walk with God to slowly slip away. We can easily do the same. Ultimately, God did speak to him again and this time Abraham said yes. If God is speaking to you again today, what will be your response?

Three

Put Your Faith Into Action

Faith: A Living, Daring Confidence in God

*H*ave you ever sensed God calling you, perhaps to leave your comfortable cocoon where you feel competent and in control, to venture into unknown territory? After calling Abraham to follow Him, God didn't forget the rest of us. He still calls today, because He has definite plans for you and me—if we're tuned in to His voice and willing to respond in faith.

Answering the telephone one day, I sensed God's voice behind the following invitation: "Poppy," asked the adviser to my Bible Study Fellowship class, "would you give the class lecture in four weeks?"

For someone else this request might have been one small step. For me, it was a giant leap of faith. At that time, I'd never given a speech in my life, let alone prepared a Bible message. After blurting out "yes," I swung between excitement and sheer terror. What was I thinking? How could someone like me stand up in front of 450 women who were used to a spiritual giant, a mature, articulate teacher of the Word?

My mind played the scene over and over like a video clip: the unsuspecting class waiting in eager anticipation. I get up. A gasp ripples through the group. They're thinking, *Who is this? We want our teacher!* And then I, a spiritual midget, begin to speak—it was too horrible to imagine more!

In spite of this fearful mental scene and the raging emotions it produced, I knew only God could have put me into such a situation. So I prepared as best I could. However, when the time came I thought I'd faint with fear.

Rows and rows of faces stared up at me as I stood clutching the podium for support. My mouth dried up, my upper lip stuck to my teeth, my stomach churned, and my knees shook. Despite my stage fright and an overwhelming desire to bolt, somehow I staggered through the lecture. When I finished, a woman rushed up to me and said, "You were great."

What would we do without kind friends?

Whether great or not, God was at work. That first terrifying experience became the foundation for what He had in store for me in the years ahead. Not only did I get acquainted with the nuts and bolts of teaching Scripture, I also learned:

- *God doesn't wait until we feel ready to do what He asks.* To develop our faith, He plunges us into the deep end so we'll learn to lean on Him, not on our own abilities.

- *God uses us even when we're terrified.* Faith isn't the absence of fear; it's doing what God says in spite of our fear.

- *God makes us sufficient for His plans, despite our self-doubts.* Gifts and skills need developing, but

God promises to provide what we need to succeed (Phil. 4:13).

When Abraham put his faith into action, he also learned a lot about God. For instance:

- *When God calls, He doesn't give details.* "By faith Abraham, when called to go to a place he would later receive as his inheritance, obeyed and went, even though he did not know where he was going" (Heb. 11:8). Notice that Abraham had no idea what lay ahead. Neither do we. Although he didn't know where God was leading him or what he'd encounter on the journey, this didn't stop him from taking that first step.

- *God doesn't ask us to rely on our own ideas and abilities.* Abraham wasn't told to figure out what to do or to make his own goals and objectives. He was to simply follow God's leading, one step, one day at a time. To do this required constantly choosing to put his faith in God.

- *God doesn't give up on us when we get sidetracked.* Abraham stopped halfway and could well have settled for far less than God wanted for him. We can too. Until the last chapter of your life and mine is written, the door to getting back on track with God remains open.

Faith is the key to walking with God, to experiencing His reality in everyday life. By putting your faith into action, you not only stretch yourself spiritually, you also bring glory to God. But have you ever asked yourself, "What exactly is faith? And what's so important about it?" Let's find some answers.

Faith—Fact or Fiction?

Have you ever heard someone say in a time of crisis, "You've gotta have faith" or "We must keep the faith"? Ever wanted to ask: faith in whom, in what? To some, faith is a stubborn determination to believe all will be well, regardless of the facts. This could be called the Ostrich syndrome. You know, bury your head in the sand, refuse to think any negative thoughts, and everything is sure to turn out just fine. This version of faith can also be called denial of reality, wishful thinking, or clutching at straws.

Faith as the New Testament describes it is being sure or confident of what we hope for—*but can't see* (Heb. 11:1). This does not mean faith is believing something that doesn't exist. I can't see electricity, but I know it exists, because whenever I turn on the switch, the light comes on. I can't see peace, but I experience it. My relationship with God is invisible, but its reality touches every part of my life.

Biblical faith is never a con job—an invitation to ignore our brains or take fiction as fact. Nor is biblical faith a deception, an enticement to believe a lie, as Jim and I did a few years ago.

Joining crowds of other innocents, we believed the promises given at a time-share presentation in Mexico and put our money down. After hair-pulling frustration—unable to get through on the phone and unable to exchange our unit for the ritzy ones displayed in the catalog—we decided to make a visit and get the full picture.

It didn't take long to see the problem. Disillusionment set in the moment we opened the door to our unit. Not only were the rooms run-down, we discovered that promises printed on important-looking pieces of paper were worthless. The developers had skipped town long ago—laden down with checks from the gullible.

When your faith is in people or their promises, it's only as reliable as they are.

I Believe in God

In contrast to putting our faith in fallible and even deliberately deceptive people, putting our faith in God shows the beginning of true wisdom. Christians, however, aren't the only ones who say they have faith in God.

Living in multi-ethnic Singapore for over two years taught me to dig a little deeper when I heard the word *god*. Whether Hindu, Sikh, Muslim, Buddhist, or Christian, we often use the same terminology, but carry vastly different concepts in our minds.

A highly educated Singaporean Chinese man whose friendship I value asked me, "Poppy, couldn't you believe that after Christ other enlightened ones came? That Christ was just one of many?" As a follower of an Indian guru who claims to be the Enlightened One, my friend would often talk about "God." But we both knew our beliefs were incompatible.

Many people today are searching for meaning, trying to find something more satisfying than acquiring all the toys they ever dreamed of. Men and women alike are finding that success alone can't satisfy their gnawing need for significance, to feel their lives have meaning. Prosperous baby boomers and others are seeking "God" in growing numbers. Others opt out of our culture's obsession with success by grasping at crystals, New Age therapies, and dreams of existing in previous lives. They, too, are searching for "God." But what kind of god? The one revealed in Scripture, or one conjured up out of fantasies, Eastern philosophies, or the occult?

My Faith Is Built On ... What?

The faith that launches us on a spiritual adventure begins with a personal encounter with the living God described in Scripture. In speaking to Nicodemus, Jesus said, "Flesh gives birth to flesh, but the Spirit gives birth to spirit.... 'You must be born again'" (John 3:6-7).

Without this, we can't know the God of all history, the self-existent one who invites us to walk day by day with Him.

With penetrating clarity, the writer of Hebrews points to Israel's God, declaring, "Without faith it is impossible to please God, because anyone who comes to him must believe that he exists and that he rewards those who earnestly seek him" (11:6).

Notice that faith is not optional if we want to please God. It is *absolutely essential*. We must believe He exists. This is step one. But even the demons believe this. To taste the reality of God's presence in our lives, we have to go beyond merely acknowledging that He exists. We must also believe that He is good and that He lovingly blesses and provides for those who earnestly seek Him. This truth is what keeps us steady when the waves of life threaten to knock us off our feet.

Real-Life Faith

When my friend Kathy called late one night, I knew something was wrong. "Poppy, would you pray for me and my family?" she asked. "My dad's been seriously injured on vacation. My mother said a large wave caught him, tumbling him onto his head and damaging his spinal cord. He has been flown back home and isn't expected to fully recover from his injuries."

Given Kathy's history of severe depression and attempts at suicide, I instantly felt concerned about how she would handle this new crisis. As we talked about her feelings, God impressed on me the depth of His healing in her life. "What amazes me the most," she confided, "is that my first thought was not panic or *How could God let this happen? My immediate reaction was What good is God going to bring out of this?*"

Instead of falling to pieces with shock and fear, Kathy's faith affected the way she responded to what happened. Instead of feeling panicky, Kathy had peace. Instead of blaming God, she consciously thanked Him for what He would do in and through the situation. And instead of drowning in thoughts of *Why him? Why now? Why this?* she confidently trusted God was at work. Far from being fiction or wishful thinking, Kathy's faith proved God's unseen but very real presence.

Shannon and Troy are experiencing the same truth.

Faith in the Valley

"Mom," said my daughter, Malaika, her voice breaking, "Shannon just called to say Troy has been diagnosed with cancer." I could hardly believe the news—Troy is only twenty-seven. Married for three years, he and Shannon are now united in battling a disease that has spread throughout his organs and bones—but God is giving them daily strength for this journey through the valley.

Visiting Troy in the hospital, I ignored the tears streaming down my face as I listened to my dear friend Dora, Shannon's mother, tell me the incredible love she'd observed. "When Troy throws up blood it's very frightening for him. But instead of leaving Troy with the nurse, Shannon holds him in her arms."

Dora took a deep breath and went on. "I'm so overwhelmed by the strength God is giving them both. When Shannon holds Troy, she sings choruses to him—and dear Troy tries to sing with her! She prays for him and whispers Scripture over and over in his ear when he's shaking with fear or pain. I am seeing their amazing faith acted out before my very eyes."

At the time of this writing, Shannon and Troy are still walking through the "valley of the shadow of death" —fighting the disease, but trusting in God's supernatural strength to face the unknown.

Can we still question if faith is fact or fiction? Kathy, Shannon and Troy have found God to be a refuge, a constant source of strength. They are living the truth of Psalm 94:19: "In the multitude of my (anxious) thoughts within me, Your comforts cheer *and* delight my soul!" (AMP).

Faith turns to God, knowing He hears our cries and sees our tears. Faith also believes that even though God might not remove painful circumstances, He will always be present, going through them with us.

Courage born of the conviction that God will sustain us through whatever lies ahead is also a fruit of faith. Isaiah wrote, "You will guard him *and* keep him in perfect *and* constant peace whose mind [both its inclination and its character] is stayed on You, because he commits himself to You, leans on You *and* hopes confidently in You" (26:3 AMP).

Faith is confident trust, not just mental assent to theoretical statements. It isn't another activity to add to our to-do list. Faith is our ringing affirmation that God exists and strengthens those who sincerely seek Him.

"Come," invites God. "Come, all you who are thirsty, come to the waters; and you who have no money, come, buy and eat!" (Isa. 55:1). His invitation flows from His love and desire to give us what we need—both salvation from sin and strength for life's stresses.

- Take a moment to reflect on your understanding of faith. If you were asked to give a definition, what would you say? Stretch your gray cells and jot down how you might respond.

- In the psalms, David describes God as "a shield for all who take refuge in him" (18:30). Write a brief prayer to God describing *your* faith in Him.

I Want to Walk by Faith—But How?

You wouldn't be reading this if you didn't want to grow in your experience of God, but what must happen to make this a reality? If we want to be people whose faith makes a difference in how we handle life, like Abraham we have to make choices. Ask yourself, "Am I willing to be stretched, to depend on God, to release control to Him?"

Let's see why these questions need to be faced if we want our faith to be more than mere words.

Faith Benefits From Stretching

The Bible talks about the God of all comfort, the God of mercy, and the God of grace and love, and we certainly delight in all those warm feelings of assurance that these attributes bring to mind. But— He is also the God who stretches the faith of those who walk with Him. You only have to look at Scripture to see this truth illustrated:

- Abraham was called to leave the known and move to the unknown. *He went.*

- Moses received scary instructions to go before Pharaoh and speak for God. *He spoke.*

- Rahab believed that Israel's God would keep her safe as the walls of Jericho literally crumbled down around her. *She trusted.*

- Hannah entrusted little Samuel to God, believing He would minister before the Lord despite being exposed to the corrupt behavior of Eli's sons. *He grew spiritually.*

- Ruth followed her mother-in-law, Naomi, into a foreign culture and lifestyle. *She took the risk.*

For an even broader picture of how God stretches those who follow Him, check out Hebrews 11. There we read of Noah, who put up with people who constantly ridiculed his faith as he built the ark. He'd never even seen rain, nor had he ever built so much as a canoe, yet he put his faith in what God said and went to work. That took courage, sheer hard work, and perseverance—all elements that spring from faith.

Filled with faith in God, David slew Goliath. He remembered that God enabled him to kill a lion and bear, banked on the fact that God doesn't change, and sprang into action. By stepping up to the challenge of killing Goliath, David's trust in God grew and God was glorified.

Who can forget the faith experience of Daniel and his three friends as they faced a horrible death—Daniel by hungry lions and his friends by fire? What about Nehemiah, who prayed and fasted, and then dared to ask the king for permission to go back to Jerusalem and rebuild the walls? And certainly no one could forget Esther's faith demonstrated when she prepared to lay down her life, saying, "I will go to the king, even though it is against the law. And if I perish, I perish" (4:16).

Having your faith challenged and stretched is inevitable if you're serious about walking with God and being available to Him. But maybe you're thinking, like me, *I certainly admire these great men and women of faith, but personally, I'd rather know ahead of time what God has in mind. In fact, I'd feel a lot more secure about what God is up to in my life if He'd hand me a detailed map.*

At the very least, don't you wish God would give us a little more information? Like pointing out the next ten steps we should take—or maybe five, or even two? That would be so reassuring. However, as we all know, this doesn't happen. God didn't do it for Abraham, or anyone else in Scripture, and He doesn't do it for us. Do you know why? He's training us to depend on Him in every situation.

Faith Requires Dependence

Imagine God provided you with a daily schedule to follow. You'd wake up every morning and there would be your schedule for the day lying on the ground, just like the manna God gave the Israelites. Would you still feel a need to consult or depend on Him? Or ask Him what to do or how to handle a situation? If you're like me, probably not.

The reason God doesn't act like some computer in the sky spitting out directions is because He is a Person who wants to relate to each of us. He alone knows what you face at work today, or the discouragement that creeps over you, or the unexpected family argument that sours your time together. And He alone can bring to your mind truths that will steady your thinking and renew your hope.

Take Susan, for instance. She has spent her life depending on others. Her mother told her what to do, and didn't stop even after she was married. For thirty years Susan leaned on Jerry, her husband, until he walked out, leaving her emotionally and financially destitute.

"I wish I could wake up in the morning and find everything is just a bad dream," she confided, "but Jerry's told me he isn't coming back and that I'd better get used to it." For the first time in her life, Susan must learn to depend on God to literally provide for her emotional and physical needs. And she is.

In a recent note, she told of friends sending her money for the down payment on a small apartment. A church acquaintance offered to adopt her dog. Another invited Susan to consult with her attorney husband. Even Susan's grown son gave her groceries. God is providing—but even more than meeting her practical needs, God is showing Susan how she can depend on Him for the wisdom and direction she needs every day. "The Lord is good, a refuge in times of trouble. He cares for those who trust in him" (Nah. 1:7). When we choose to depend, we choose to grow—and the God who is trustworthy receives the praise.

Faith for right now comes when you take a deep breath and remind your heart that God is in control. When circumstances tempt you to cry out, "I can't handle this," you have a choice. Will you listen to those little inner tapes tempting you to panic, or to God's Word that teaches you to trust?

Imagine if God never permitted anything to touch your safe, comfortable cocoon. Or if He never invited you to attempt something beyond what you can do under your own steam, something that proved His power. Would you ever know what *He* could make you capable of? No. Your experience of God's reality would always remain secondhand, anemic, an unreal daydream.

Yes, putting our faith into action *is* often a struggle. But think of the exciting results when we learn to depend on God rather than on our own self-assessment. We'll not only see His glory, we'll also see our own growth shining through.

Faith Requires Our Releasing Control

When God first appeared to Abraham, His command had much greater significance than a mere request to relocate. At its core, God's call was a test of Abraham's willingness to release control of his own destiny. Knowing the eternal purposes He had in mind, God challenged Abraham to take his hands off his own life.

Isn't this what God asks of us?

One afternoon in the early years of my walk with God, the issue of releasing control drove me to my knees. Along with several hundred other women attending a weekend retreat, I took my sheet of questions to a quiet place where I could spend an uninterrupted hour with God.

One question jumped out at me: "Is there anything you will not do for the Lord?" Immediately I knew what God was saying. Would I deliberately step back into an incredibly painful situation if He asked me to? I began to cry and pray at the same time. "God, I can't do that; please don't ask it of me." As I remained in His presence, however, God brought me to a place of releasing my will and the determination to control this area of my life.

In the school of faith, this is one lesson God teaches over and over. Relinquishing control establishes Christ as Lord. By entrusting our well-being to Him, who wants only our good, we can have peace.

In case you're wondering, God didn't ask me to do what I dreaded. However, there have been other times when He did ask me to relinquish my desires, priorities, or "rights." Being willing to uncurl our tight grip on what we want, when it isn't God's best for us at that time, is part of going deeper with God.

Spiritual progress doesn't happen without being stretched, depending on God, and releasing control to Him. Understanding this is essential. What's the result? You see God come through for you.

Your faith moves from "Well, I hope God will help me" to "God has helped me, and I know He'll be there for me, whatever comes." Instead of theory, your experience of God's faithfulness becomes a powerful motivator to greater growth.

Let me encourage you to stop for a few minutes and review your own faith experiences. Maybe you've sensed God calling you to speak up for your beliefs when a co-worker or relative scorned your faith. Perhaps you learned to trust Him when your world collapsed around you—your husband left, your child rebelled, or your dreams lay smashed. Or perhaps you stepped into a new situation, believing that was God's will for you. You were scared, but so dependent on God you felt buoyed up, as if He were constantly infusing joy and confidence into you.

- If you recall a time when you grew spiritually because God stretched your faith, taught you to depend on Him, or challenged you to release control, take a moment and record it. This is an important part of your spiritual history.

- Take another look at those times when God stretched your faith. How did *He* receive glory from what happened, either in the situation or in your walk with Him?

- Although it's encouraging to look back and see God's faithfulness, we can't live on spiritual nostalgia. Walking with God is a present activity—it's for today, and the struggles, confusion, and fears we face *now*. Ask yourself, "How am I handling what's stressing me out today? Am I looking to God to provide what I need—or am I still relying on my own resources?" Take this moment of honesty to record your thoughts, and then give God what's troubling you right now.

Faith Blockers—Faith Builders

A course description for "Walking With God 101" might read, "Take your hands off your life and let God direct your path." Instead of doing this, however, we often wrestle with what God impresses on us. We wonder if He knows what He's asking. We question His wisdom. We shrink from the assignment He calls us to. We want to stay exactly where we are and not take any action. The result? Missed opportunities to experience God at work in powerful ways.

Have you ever wondered *why* we react like this? Or *what* blocks our willingness to act in faith? See if you identify with these common reasons:

Faith Blockers

- **Ignorance of God.** We don't know much about God's character or promises, or we haven't experienced the thrill of seeing Him work on our behalf.

- **Inward Focus on:** *Our resources*—we look at the situation counting only on our own abilities.
  Our fears—we fixate on failure, and allow defeating thoughts to take over.
  Our agenda—we judge whether or not we want to do what God asks.

- **Insufficient Expectations.** We don't think to ask God to act on our behalf, or we question what difference He can make.

Much could be said about these faith blockers, but let's change our focus to the positive.

How can we strengthen our faith? Rather than minutely examining how much or how little we have, let's ask ourselves, "Where am I putting my faith? In my own abilities, education, quick thinking, or personality? In people I know? In someone who can smooth the way? In what strings I can pull? Or in trusting God?"

Our human tendency is to take charge. Forgetting about God, we instinctively depend on our own strengths and resources to tackle whatever comes. Yet God wants us to grow in faith, build our reliance on Him, and experience His power in our lives. This only happens when we cultivate the habit of inviting Him into every situation. When we don't, the results are simply what we brought about by our own efforts, however successful. This will be explained more fully in a later chapter.

To experience God at work, our faith has to be a living reality, not an impractical theory. The fact that God exists and is active today needs to seep into every part of our thinking. When it does, our response to what happens in our lives changes.

You might not feel you have much faith right now, but faith is like a spiritual muscle that can be strengthened and built up. I know, because I'm working on it myself.

To help you develop a stronger faith in God, here are three exercises that have helped Christians down through the ages. Practice them regularly, and then watch yourself learning to depend on God rather than on your own resources.

Faith Builders

- **Seek a Closer Relationship With God.** Treat yourself to chunks of time in the evening or on your lunch hour to read the Bible. Observe how God worked in people's lives and how they showed either faith or unbelief. Read slowly through Abraham's story or see what you can learn from Elijah in 1 Kings 17-19. Dig into Christian biographies. These exciting stories about God coming through for people just like us are sure to stretch and strengthen your faith. If you don't know where to begin, ask a friend, pastor, or inquire at a Christian bookstore.

- **Take Time to Pray.** In the morning, ask God to remind you all day long that He is with you, whatever comes. Then when something unexpected does come, train yourself to say, "Lord, I give this to you. I know you can handle this so I'm putting my trust in you. If there's something you want me to do, Lord, show me. If not, help me to stand back while you sort it out."

- **Set Your Eyes on God.** We're told to set, or fix, our eyes on Jesus for a good reason. If we set them on how impossible a situation is, how we can't handle it, how we don't know where we will turn if this or that happens, we'll drown in doubt and despair. Feed faith by setting your eyes, your thoughts, and your trust, on *what God can do*, not on what you can't do. Faith grows out of choosing to either look inward and groan or look upward and grow.

- **See Yourself As Significant to God.** When you question, "Will God help me? Will He work things out for good? Does He love me and see me as precious?" Tell yourself, Yes, He does! I am God's child, I am in Christ, I have the Holy Spirit within me. I am dearly loved by Him." What you tell yourself etches grooves in your mind. Fill those grooves with biblical truth to help your faith and courage grow.

Choosing to Leave ... and Go

Throughout our journey, God's Spirit urges us to cling closer to Him, to come up higher. He whispers, "Walk by faith" when life seems out of control. "Put your trust in me" when you can't change someone you deeply love. "Draw your strength from me right now, today, in this situation you're facing," when you're wrestling with fear. All difficult circumstances, of every kind, offer opportunities to cultivate our faith and expand our ever-growing experience of trusting God. This was as true for Abraham as it is for us.

Abraham proved his faith by leaving where he was in order to go where God directed. The call to "Leave ... and go" applies to our walk also; perhaps not always geographically, but emotionally and spiritually (Gen. 12:1).

To walk with Him, God calls us to leave behind whatever holds us back. "Throw off everything that hinders and the sin that so easily entangles ... run with perseverance the race marked out for us ... strengthen your feeble arms and weak knees ... see that you do not refuse him who speaks," commands the writer of Hebrews in chapter 12.

This might require leaving your comfortable cocoon to step into something new, even scary. It might mean discarding damaging attitudes you have toward yourself, or someone else, because they're hindering your spiritual progress. Perhaps God's call to you is to throw off fear, or self-centeredness, or spiritual apathy.

The call of God varies with the "land" we're dwelling in—but it is always to go forward toward His best for us. His goal is to see us mature and become a blessing to others.

- Is this what you desire? If so, is there some area in your life God is asking you to leave behind? Is there a new "land" He wants you to move into? Perhaps writing your thoughts as a prayer will help you follow through on what God is saying.

- The psalmist prayed, "O my God, I trust, lean on, rely on *and* am confident in You" (25:2 AMP). Can you say this? If so, how is your faith in God making a difference in what's happening in your life today?

Daily Choices for the Growing Heart
Put Your Faith Into Action

Choose to see every situation as an opportunity to cultivate your faith. This attitude will turn your life into a spiritual adventure.

- *By faith:* Believe God is at work in you, even if your life feels chaotic.

- *By faith:* Trust God to give you poise and clear thinking in stressful situations.

- *By faith:* Count on God to stir the heart or conscience of someone you're praying for.

- *By faith:* Look to Him, asking that He satisfy the needs you have right now.

- Expect God to act—and watch to see the mysterious ways He'll work on your behalf. Take your faith off its theological shelf and apply it to life. Instead of wondering how you can do what God asks, choose to believe God will make you adequate. This is all-out trust. Let your faith make a practical difference today.

Four

Count on God's Promise

God's promises are like the stars.
The darker the night, the brighter they shine.[1]

*L*inda was stressed out.

"I'm preparing a team to work with children this summer," she said, when I asked how she was doing. "Several of the people have never worked with kids before, so this means more intensive training from me. Also, their mix of personalities adds to the challenge.

"In addition," Linda continued, "when John and I bought a fixer-upper house recently, I thought it wouldn't add much stress. Well, was I ever wrong! Plus, our previous house is still sitting on the market. I lie awake at night wondering how we're going to manage. Another area that's overwhelming is my job. It seems as though I'm forever behind." She paused to shake her head, adding, "I've just got to get caught up before I take time off for the outreach to children."

Feeling swamped and barely able to survive happens to most of us. Who hasn't occasionally wanted to yell, "Stop the world! I want to get off"? I know I have. But the world doesn't stop its demands no matter how stressed we feel.

I could see Linda's needs: wisdom to handle the personalities on her team, peace as she faced a torn-up house and two mortgages, and stamina to get caught up at work. I promised to pray—and I did. Thinking about her the next day, I found myself asking, "Lord, give me something to share that will turn her focus away from feeling overwhelmed. Is there some promise or specific truth that would calm her down and encourage her to have confidence in you?"

Soon after I prayed, my mind churned with remembered promises: "I will not forget you. See, I have engraved you on the palms of my hands," and "The eternal God is your refuge, and underneath are the everlasting arms." Now they came faster, "Those who hope in the Lord will renew their strength," then, "[He] is able to do immeasurably more than all we ask or imagine, according to his power that is at work within us," and others (Isa. 49:15-16; Deut. 33:27; Isaiah 40:31; Eph. 3:20).

I dashed off a short e-mail with these verses, assuring Linda of my continued prayers. She knows, and so do I, that her situation won't change quickly. By fixing her mind on God's promises, though, her perspective most definitely will.

Standing on the Promises

A pastor tells the story of getting into trouble with his mother when he was a boy. Coming into his bedroom one night, his mother found him standing on his Bible. In response to her horrified question, "What are you doing?" he replied, "Mom, I'm standing on the promises of God, like we sing about in church." If we want to stand, not literally, but figuratively, on the promises of God, we need to know something about them.

What Is a Promise?

Stemming from the root word *angel*, meaning "to proclaim, announce, declare," a promise is a "public declaration which must come true in order to be believed."[2] The Bible contains over three thousand promises, according to some sources. Many of these promises relate to the nation of Israel and God's divine purposes for them as a people. Other promises point to the life of Christ, His second coming, the indwelling of the Holy Spirit, and how God lovingly works in the lives of His children.

Down through the centuries people have made promises to whatever "gods" they worshiped. They beg, plead, sacrifice, and desperately cry out for help. But their deaf "gods" make no promises to them. In contrast, look through the Bible and notice this: The God of Scripture makes promises to us. He presents himself as One who loves, takes an intimate interest in, and actively works on our behalf.

Are God's Promises Reliable?

People make and break promises so easily today, it's little wonder we're tempted at times to question God's reliability. Before we trust anyone, it's smart to check out the person's track record. Does he keep his word or doesn't he? Does she make grandiose promises but fail to live up to them? These are not only valid questions to ask about people—but about God, too. After all, trust is essential for believing anyone's promises. So if we want to feel confident about counting on God's promises, we clearly need to check God's track record.

To do this, let's consider:

- The Bible's claims about God's character
- What history has proven
- Personal experience

The Bible's Claims:

"God is not a man that he should lie, nor a son of man, that he should change his mind. Does he speak and then not act? Does he promise and not fulfill?" (Num. 23:19). Scripture after Scripture affirms the exact opposite: Our God has unlimited power. No force exists that can stop Him from carrying out what He promises to do. Speaking through Isaiah, God declares, "My purpose will stand, and I will do all that I please.... What I have said, that will I bring about; what I have planned, that will I do" (46:10-11).

The Bible also claims God knows everything. He knows what will happen an hour, day or a year from now. Because of this, He never has to break a promise because of unexpected circumstances—which most of us mere mortals have had to do.

Another assertion made about God is that He is faithful. This is one of His attributes. If this weren't true, He could never be described as good, holy, or all-powerful. Affirming God's trustworthiness and dependability, the apostle Paul declares, "The one who calls you is faithful and *he will do it*" (1 Thess. 5:24).

With this brief look at what the Bible claims, let's see what happened.

History Has Proven:

God promised to give Abraham a son. *He did.*

God promised to make Abraham into a great nation. *He did.*

God promised to give Abraham's offspring the land. *He did.*

God promised blessings for obedience and punishment for rebellion. *This happened.*

God promised a Messiah, a Savior. *He came.*

Jesus promised the Holy Spirit would come. *He did.*

God promised His Word would bear fruit. *It does.*

God's track record can never be completely listed by a human being. Only He knows all the ways He has kept His promises down through history. What we can observe for ourselves, however, are the personal experiences of men and women in Scripture—and of those living today. Let's look at a few of these.

Personal Experience:

Someone has said that faith feeds on the promises of God. How true. Elijah believed God's promises and boldly declared to King Ahab there would be no rain until he, Elijah, said so. After this God helped him get out of town, telling him where to hide and promising him airborne supplies of food, morning and evening. This worked well until his personal drinking fountain dried up. Then God gave him more instructions and promises.

Instead of camping out in a ravine all by himself, Elijah was now instructed to head for a distant town and look for a particular woman, a widow. Upon spotting her, Elijah requested a drink of water, and then decided to also ask for a piece of bread. Turning on him, the widow told Elijah sharply that she had only enough flour to make something for herself and her son. A cup of water was one thing, but there certainly wasn't enough food to share with him.

Elijah responded gently, but insistently. He told her she was to do what he said—and count on Gods promise that the jar of flour will not be used up and the jug of oil will not run dry until the day the Lord gives rain on the land" (1 Kings 17:14). Did God keep His promise to this single mother in Zarephath? Read the story and find out (1 Kings 17:7-16).

Remember Jesus' promise of everlasting water to the Samaritan woman? Did she get what He promised? How about Jesus' promise to Martha at the tomb of Lazarus? He said that if she'd believe, she'd see the glory of God. Isn't that what happened when Lazarus stumbled out, wrapped in his burial clothes? And what about Jesus' promise to the woman who poured perfume over His head, only to be promptly criticized by everyone—except Jesus. Acknowledging her devotion and deep insight into what lay before Him, Jesus promised that her act would be remembered forever. So far, His promise has lasted two thousand years.

Promises and Principles

In studying and meditating on specific promises made to individuals in Scripture, it's important to remember that those actual promises might not be ours to claim. What we can do, however, is count on the spiritual principle hidden in that specific promise.

This is what Danielle did as she looked at the mountain of work stacked up on her desk. A relaxing vacation followed by a migraine had kept her out of the office longer than she'd planned. "I have twenty-three hours of work to cram into eight hours," she said.

With a wry smile creasing her tanned face, she continued, "I was just reading this morning about Elijah and that widow who had so little food. What struck me was how few resources I have to meet all the demands on me today. Knowing I'm no different than her, and God hasn't changed, I prayed, 'God, I'm giving you all the energy and ideas I have, and I'm going to trust you to supply me with what I need. *Thank you for what you're going to do.*'"

By thinking about what she was reading, Danielle found a spiritual principle that applied to her circumstances. She understood that God doesn't change; therefore, neither do the spiritual principles by which He operates. He promises to supply our need just as He met the need of the widow of Zarephath—provided we give Him what we have.

As you read about people's lives in Scripture, look for life lessons. Try to find examples of God keeping His promises. Watch for spiritual principles that you can claim. Don't forget: The stories given in Scripture are not there simply for our information; they are given for our transformation.

For another example of God's reliability, consider Peggy's story. Feeling discouraged and trapped in a church that was torn with factions and gossip, Peggy pleaded with her husband, Frank, to leave the church, but he refused. His roots there ran deep, and as far as he was concerned, Peggy should ignore her feelings and get over it.

Feeling more and more discouraged, Peggy found herself thinking that not even God could change Frank's heart. She felt hopeless and doomed to stay—until the day God's Spirit revealed what she was telling herself. Challenging her unbelief, she sensed God saying, *"Is anything too hard for the Lord?"* Gasping at what she'd allowed herself to think, Peggy cried out, "No, Lord! Nothing. Absolutely nothing is too hard for you. Forgive me for doubting your power to do whatever is your will. I'm going to believe you can do this. And I'm going to pray and believe that nothing is too hard for you."

A month after this spiritual crisis, having prayed earnestly day by day and choosing to believe God could do the impossible, Peggy and Frank left that church and never went back. Unknown to Peggy, Frank had also been wrestling with some church issues, but kept his thoughts to himself. When she told him she simply couldn't continue going, Frank chose to leave with her.

My friend, think back on what you've just read, putting yourself in the shoes of each person. Their situations seemed impossible, but God came through for them. I don't know what impossible situation is burdening your heart today, but whatever you're struggling with, be assured—God does keep His promises.

- God promises to give you what He knows you need—
  not only today but also in the days to come. Will you
  choose to believe what He says, based on His claims and
  track record? If this is hard for you, take a moment to
  express your thoughts and feelings to Him.

If you want to count on God's promises, make some time to
search the Word. Ask Him to bring a promise to mind. When He
does, repeat it over and over to yourself throughout the day—believe
it, count on it, and feed your faith on what God has said. He won't
fail you.

"Standing on the promises of God" isn't some quaint notion left
over from an old hymn; it's a dynamic truth waiting to be put to the
test in whatever circumstances you face.

Can I Have Anything I Ask?

"As a new Christian I fell madly in love with a certain guy," said
Courtney. "I didn't know much about the Bible, but when I found the
verse 'Delight yourself in the Lord and he will give you the desires of
your heart,' I immediately decided this was God's promise that Tom
would fall for me. I claimed that verse for a long time, but nothing
ever happened. Now that I've grown spiritually, I realize the desire of
my heart at that time wasn't exactly God-centered. Looking at some
of the choices Tom made later in life, and how God's blessed me with
my husband, Jack, I'm glad I didn't get what I pleaded for."

Can we have anything we want from God? Obviously not. Before
we simply claim something that appeals to us, we need to consider
several factors:

Does the Promise Have Conditions?

Courtney didn't even consider this. We can make the same mistake when we read Jesus' words "You may ask me for anything in my name, and I will do it" (John 14:14). Sounds good, doesn't it?

However, before you think Jesus' promise is like a credit card offering unlimited access to whatever your heart desires, take a look at the previous verse: "I will do whatever you ask in my name, so that the Son may bring glory to the Father." Both of these promises illustrate the importance of reading Scripture carefully and in context.

First, to ask in Jesus' name means that whatever we ask must be *what He would ask*—so much for our self-centered requests! Second, our motivation for asking must be *to bring glory to the Father.*

Without a doubt, God does shower us with promises that have the power to change our perspective, lift our mood, and fill us with hope—but let's not ignore the accompanying conditions.

Is My Will Yielded to God's Will?

Facing the agony of the cross, Jesus yielded His will to the Father in words that must be echoed in our lives: "Not my will but Thine be done." When life deals us any kind of blow, such as a broken relationship, a lost job, a death in the family, or a frightening illness, we understandably cry out to God and claim various promises. Hard as it is, however, we must look at Scripture in its total teaching, not just at those promises that seem to hold out hope for escape.

In this life, trials and heartaches come to those who don't call God their Father *as well as to those who do.* His promises never state we won't go through the valley of tears or the valley of death. To claim on the basis of God's promises that it's possible to go through life without any suffering is to fly in the face of Scripture and reality.

What the promises do hold out to us is the steady assurance that God's strength and comfort are available for every trial: *"When* you pass through the waters ... the rivers ... the fire ... I will be with you" (Isa. 43:2, paraphrased).

Have I Confessed All Known Sin?

In addition to checking out these factors, we also must come to grips with any disobedience in our lives. Most of us would rather forget this requirement, but it has to be faced. Let's be honest. Our human tendency is to want God to keep His promises to us while letting us keep our pet sins. This isn't how spiritual growth works.

If we're going to walk with Him, we need to both *know* and *practice* James 4:7-10: "Submit yourselves, then, to God. Resist the devil, and he will flee from you. Come near to God, and he will come near to you. Wash your hands ... purify your hearts ... grieve, mourn and wail.... Humble yourselves before the Lord, and he will lift you up." That's strong stuff.

There's no way we can miss what James is saying—Christians are to take sin seriously. But God doesn't focus on our sin only. Did you notice His command is accompanied by a promise? If you humble yourself—*He will lift you up.*

Check God's Commands for His Promises

"God's commands are not always accompanied by reasons," says F. B. Meyer, British writer and preacher, "but always by promises, expressed or understood."[3]

When you're reading the Word and come across a command, look for the promise that goes with it. God doesn't say, "You do this," without also saying, "I will do that." Even though Scripture does have many commands, they're given for our good. The promises attached to them not only motivate us to obey, they say something positive will happen if we do. This makes sense because God's intention is to encourage us to walk closely with Him—to draw near, not rebel and run the other way.

See how this powerful principle works:

1. Paul instructs: "Live by the Spirit." The promise? "You will not gratify the desires of the sinful nature" (Gal. 5:16).

2. Jesus repeatedly stated, "Do not worry." The underlying principle and promise? You are more valuable to God than birds or flowers. He knows what you need. He will take care of you (Matt. 6:25-34).

3. The writer of Hebrews commands: "Keep your lives free from the love of money and be content with what you have." The accompanying promise? "Never will I leave you; never will I forsake you" (13:5).

Part of walking with God is learning that His commands aren't always accompanied by reasons we can understand, or want to accept. But they do come with loving promises. Abraham learned this as soon as he started to move toward God.

While living in Haran, Abraham's understanding of walking with God was far more limited than what we enjoy today. We have his story, plus countless others, as well as the teachings of the New Testament to guide us. How much he grasped, we don't know. Having the sensitivity to hear and obey God in Ur, we can safely assume he was sensitive to his halfhearted obedience in Haran. Certainly he knew God's blessings and promises had been put on hold.

Throwing off the spiritual stagnation that bogged down his progress, Abraham finally left Haran—and his life promptly began to change. Now that he had fully obeyed, God considered him ready to receive all He had been waiting to give.

Pouring out a wealth of awe-inspiring promises, God declared over and over, "I will bless you ... I will make you...." Abraham must have been left speechless—and no doubt longed to get to know this One who had broken into his life. God's promises forever changed Abraham's view of himself, his future, and the significance of his life. God's promises can have the same effect on us—if we allow them to work in our lives.

- Think about your life right now—your job, family, friends, health, finances. What would you like the Lord to do? Jot down what's on your heart.

- If you know a promise that relates to your need, write it down as best you can remember it. How does this verse encourage you? Try to be specific.

- Have you checked if there's a condition attached? What is God urging and prompting you to do about it?

Promises—The Proof of God's Love.

God's promises are a constantly available source of encouragement. Not only do specific promises give us hope and determination to carry on, all of them tell us something about how God feels toward us. Just think about the glorious abundance and variety of promises in the Bible—isn't that in itself evidence that God loves and deeply cares for us? Don't all these promises shout beyond a doubt how significant and precious we are to Him? Isn't their very existence a constant reminder that when life is tough, both the weak and the tough can turn to Him for help?

God's promises to Abraham were specific and encouraging, revealing His divine plan. We've also been given promises that are specific and encouraging—promises that reveal God's divine plans for our lives. Out of the thousands of promises we can count on, God says the same things to us that He said to Abraham: I will make you fruitful, I will bless you, and I will make you a blessing.

Let's look at some of the promises God made to Abraham that profoundly changed the direction and fulfillment of his life—and at three promises that can change the direction and fulfillment of ours.

I Will ...

Gods Specific Promise to Abraham

"I will make you into a great nation" (Gen. 12:2). What a promise to make to a seventy-five-year-old man who had no children—but Abraham was "fully persuaded that God had power to do what he had promised" (Rom. 4:21). As the years went by, Abraham's faith was tested over and over as God expanded on the promise many more times.

He declared, "All the land that you see I will give to you and your offspring forever.... If anyone could count the dust, then your offspring could be counted" (Gen. 13:15-16). God stretched Abraham's faith for twenty-five years. He didn't waver in his conviction that God would keep His word—even though there was no sign of it happening. What faith! Does it encourage you, as it does me, to keep on praying for the deepest longings of your heart?

In His divine plan to reveal himself to humankind, God chose Abraham to be the father of a nation, Israel. Physically speaking, it seemed impossible. In all those years, no evidence appeared that his life would ever bear fruit—and yet God promised it would be so. Abraham *would* reproduce; he *would* experience God's mighty power flowing through his life.

"Against all hope, Abraham in hope believed and so became the father of many nations, just as it had been said to him.... He did not waver through unbelief regarding the promise of God" (Rom. 4:18, 20).

God's Promise to Us

"Whoever lives in me and I in him shall produce a large crop of fruit" (John 15:5 TLB). Abraham isn't the only person God intended to be fruitful. Fruitfulness is for you and for me, too. True, there are those days when we might feel the only fruit we're bearing is sour grapes, but Jesus does make a promise we can count on. Notice, though, the condition for fruitfulness.

To bear spiritual fruit—whether seeing ourselves change or being part of God's work in someone else—requires living in Christ and allowing Him to live His life through us. This can seem rather mystical and difficult to grasp. Different Bible versions use the words *remain, abide, live.* They're each saying the same thing: In order to bear spiritual fruit, we need to stay close to Christ—talking to Him, listening to Him, and doing His will.

A little apple is not going to grow into a delicious, nutrient-filled fruit if it gets detached from the branch. Nor will we produce a large crop of spiritual fruit if, under the pressure of other priorities, we fail to stay spiritually attached to the source of our growth, Jesus Christ. Jesus made this clear: "Apart from me you can't do a thing" (John 15:5 TLB). Fruit isn't produced by our efforts; it comes as a result of our being attached to Christ. He is the One who makes fruit happen; He is the Vine.

When we take time to be with Him—thinking about what He's saying to us and letting praise and gratitude and love flow into our hearts—we're abiding, remaining, living close to Him. Jesus' promise then comes true—we bear fruit. It can't be stopped, because this is His life flowing out of us. When you realize you're showing patience instead of making a snippy remark, releasing a hurt rather than growing it into a grudge, or speaking warmly to a co-worker instead of ignoring her presence—you're bearing fruit, just as Jesus promised.

On those days when you feel you don't have much value in God's great cosmic plan, don't despair. Instead, remember what Jesus said: "I chose you and appointed you to go and bear fruit—fruit that will last" (John 15:16). Not only does God know you, you matter to Him. He has plans to bless your life, just as He blessed Abraham.

God's Specific Promise to Abraham

"I will bless you (Gen. 12:2). God didn't make promises to Abraham as if He were a company president offering a benefits package in return for loyal service. He committed to personally blessing Abraham, enriching his life and providing for all his needs. Entering into a person-to-person friendship with Abraham, God continued to reveal who He was, how He thought, and what His plans were—just as any close friend does.

This wasn't a one-sided relationship in which Abraham kept reaching out to a remote being. God *cultivated* their friendship. Making himself known to Abraham at various times, God talked with him when he was scared and discouraged, confused, or in need of assurance. He freely promised to be Abraham's shield of protection in the midst of trouble, and his great reward. In declaring "I will bless you," God guaranteed Abraham that all his needs would be supplied—so long as he looked to Him every step of the way.

God's Promise to Us

"We have all benefited from the rich blessings he brought to us— blessing upon blessing heaped upon us!" (John 1:16 TLB). God's promises have brought us more blessings than we can possibly recall. Here are just a few of the spiritual blessings we've received:

- We have a person-to-person relationship with the living God.

- We have access to God's help. In fact, we're told to "approach the throne of grace with confidence, so that we may receive mercy and find grace to help in our time of need" (Heb. 4:16).

- We can cry Abba—Daddy—Father, knowing He hears and cares (Rom. 8:15-16).

- We have the ability to stand against the devil's schemes (Eph. 6:10-18).

- He promises to bear our burdens, free us from worry and anxiety, protect us, make all things work for our good, and empower us to live a supernatural life.

- We've received forgiveness, acceptance, wisdom, direction, mercy, and kindness—even the very embrace of God (Eph. 1:3-14).

The list of God's blessings is endless—no wonder we're told to count them one by one. Because God is love, He gives—this is His nature. And we're the recipients. No fortune of any kind can compare with what we've been given in our relationship with God. He was not only Abraham's very great reward, He is also yours and mine.

God's Specific Promise to Abraham

"I will make your name great, and you will be a blessing" (Gen. 12:2). Some people's names are instantly recognized but totally repugnant. The names of Judas, Stalin, Hitler, and Idi Amin easily come to mind. The name of Abraham is equally recognizable, but what a contrast. He is revered as "the father of many nations," honored as a "mighty prince," respected as "a prophet," and followed as "a man of faith" (Gen. 17:5; 23:6; 20:7; Gal. 3:9).

Starting out as an obscure, insignificant middle-aged man, Abraham walked with God in such a way that his name became great—both in his time and down through history. He knew God promised his name would be great, yet we don't find him manipulating behind the scenes to make this happen. Nor did he throw his weight around, demanding special treatment because God had singled him out for great blessing. What a tribute to his character.

Although Abraham became a man of power and wealth with the favor of God on his life, he chose to walk in humility. His heart was focused on pleasing God, not on pleasing himself or taking personal advantage of his unique privileges. God knew Abraham's failings, yet He made his name great—as He said He would.

God also kept His promise to bless every nation of the world through Abraham's offspring. Today the Bible is translated into numerous languages, the good news of Christ is heard around the world, and believers from every nation rejoice in the Lord. Yes, God keeps His promises—after all, who or what can stop the One who is eternal, unchanging, and all-powerful?

God's Promise to Us

"Those who honor me I will honor" (1 Sam. 2:30). Have you ever heard of the Shilluck people? Neither had I, until I read about their faith in a mission magazine.[4] The Shilluck people live in the Sudan, an African country ripped apart by civil war. Not only are people in this region dying because of the fighting, they are also starving to death because of an ongoing famine.

Some of our Shilluck brothers and sisters in Christ live in a refugee camp where they receive just enough food to survive. In spite of this, responding to the challenge given by their national pastors to be good stewards, they are giving to the Lord out of the little they have.

Believing God's promise to supply their needs if they would trust Him, each family in the congregation sets aside a spoonful of sugar or a handful of flour whenever they make tea or cook a meal. This is Jesus' portion. On Sundays the families joyfully bring their offering, which is then sold in Monday's market. In this way, they're raising money to pay their pastors, complete their church buildings, and assist the needy.

What a way to honor God! In turn, He's honoring them by supplying their needs and making their name great. Not only are they experiencing God's blessings, they're also being a blessing to all who hear of their faith and love.

Do you want to be honored by God and be a blessing to others like the Shillucks? You can be. God says when you and I honor Him, He honors us. Jesus honored the Father by being a servant—and He calls us to follow in His footsteps. This is our calling and our privilege—to meet the needs of others, even if doing so means missing our favorite

TV show, costing us financially, or cutting into our plans for the weekend.

Share who you are and what you have with someone in need, and God will honor you because you're honoring Him with your obedience. And guess what? Your name will be great with God and with those who thank God for you. You'll be both a blessing and blessed. That's God's promise.

Daily Choices for the Growing Heart
Count on God's Promise

After receiving God's promises, Abraham knew his life would never be the same. Neither will yours, once you understand and count on what God says.

To reap the benefits God intends for you:

- Collect them—just as you collect figurines, china cups, or teaspoons.

- Record them—title a page in a notebook or journal "God's Promises." Whenever you come across a promise from reading your Bible, a book, or listening to a sermon, write it down along with the reference.

- Seek them—ask friends for promises they've counted on when going through difficult times.

- Claim them—choose one from your list every time you present a need to the Lord.

What will God's promises do? They'll jump-start your faith, calm you down, assure you of His loving control, and flash reminders of who He is and how much you matter to Him. Get familiar with them, count on them, and then get ready to see your walk with God come alive.

Five

Trust God in Confusing Circumstances

Trusting God is not a matter of my feelings but of my will.[1]

"God," I pleaded, "please send someone to help me. I'm so lost, and everyone will be wondering what happened to their speaker." With the sun rapidly sinking, and no cars, road signs, or houses in sight, I continued, "Lord, if you don't rescue me, I'm going to be driving around all night. HELP!"

Zipping off to remote retreat centers hidden in the vast forests of the Northwest is not one of my favorite activities. Neither is following skimpy and confusing maps.

Staring intently down the ruler-straight road cut between miles of identical fir trees, I looked for some miraculous answer to my prayer. Surely God would send some sign—maybe a pillar of fire or a bright star to guide me. There was nothing—at least for a few seconds. Catching my breath, I watched almost in disbelief. Pulling out from a side road about half a mile ahead, a blue police car turned in the direction I was headed and started to accelerate.

Feeling like an Indy 500 race-car driver, I pushed on the gas and drove as fast as I could. Flashing my lights and beeping my horn, for once in my life I prayed a police officer would look in his rearview mirror and see me. He did.

Recognizing a damsel in distress, the officer showed suitable concern. "Yes, ma'am," he responded in answer to my panicky questions. "I know the retreat center you're trying to find, but you're miles off course and headed in the wrong direction. Why don't you follow me and I'll lead you there?" What a relief.

I was tempted to ask him what he was doing in the woods, but thought better of it. After all, it wasn't really my business to inquire if he was chasing a crazed serial killer or merely taking a little nap. "God caused him to appear when you were totally confused, and that's all you need to know" I told my naturally curious self.

Singing joyfully at the top of my lungs for the next half hour, I followed my knight in a shining blue car, completely confident he knew where I was supposed to go, even if I didn't. Crunching to a stop at the retreat center's driveway, my rescuer pointed out the sign and sped off. I had arrived at my destination—having found, once again, that God can be trusted.

When Abraham set off to travel through the Promised Land, he didn't possess any kind of map—skimpy or otherwise. Nor did a state patrolman appear from behind a sand dune to point the way. Instead, our hero simply trusted God to tell him where to go and what to do.

Not knowing what he'd encounter, he set his heart to follow God. In turn, God set himself to develop Abraham's character and faith. Using external circumstances—the Canaanites in the land, a famine, and no son or heir—God went to work on the awesome transformation of Abraham into a man of faith. Abraham had to learn to trust, believe, and to walk in obedience, no matter the cost. Only then could God use his life to bless the world.

God's goals and methods haven't changed. He yearns to use our lives to bless others. For this to happen, we need our character and faith developed just as Abraham did. One of the tools God uses to accomplish His work in us is external circumstances—those times of confusion, stress, and pain. In those situations where we don't know what to do, where we struggle with fear, are overwhelmed with doubts, or swamped by grief, we learn the same faith lessons as Abraham did.

What did Abraham learn? Exactly what we need to learn if we're to grow in trust:

- God's character is the foundation of our trust.
- Confusing circumstances are opportunities to trust.
- Cultivating worship strengthens our ability to trust.
- Crises of faith reveal whom we trust.

God's Character--The Foundation for Our Trust

Life rarely unfolds in exactly the way we expect or want it to. Sometimes people aren't what they seem. Even when we're walking in God's will as best we know how, the unexpected and unwanted happens. We need to know and accept these facts, even while we wish they weren't true. Unless we understand and accept that walking with God doesn't guarantee a pain-free life, our trust in Him is going to be severely shaken.

Elisabeth Elliot, referring to the death of her first husband, Jim, along with four other missionaries, writes, "They had gone into Auca territory to take the Gospel there.... They loved God. They trusted him. They had prayed for protection, guidance, and success, and they had put their faith in him as shield and defender. As we, their wives, prayed with them over every step of the preparations for this venture, we thought surely God would protect and guide and give success."

The shocking martyrdom of her husband and friends forced Elisabeth to examine her faith. Could she trust that God was who He claimed to be: loving, kind, all-wise? She knew she had to make a choice—either to "deny God or believe Him, to trust Him or renounce Him."[2]

If we look at unfair, confusing, or horrific circumstances and judge God's character on the basis of what we see, we're going to find ourselves in an enormous spiritual and mental battle. Doesn't Scripture say God is holy, all-powerful, full of compassion? Then how could He have allowed this? Judging God even further, we're tempted to accuse Him of being cruel, capricious, or callously indifferent. What other conclusion can we come to?

When such powerful emotions wash over us, struggling with our beliefs is normal. God doesn't condemn us because we wrestle with what He permits. He knows we can't figure out His ways. How could we? We're mere finite human beings unable to fathom divine mysteries.

Where do these painful issues that we all face leave us? With two choices. As Elisabeth Elliot stated, will we deny and renounce God, or will we believe and trust Him, in spite of the evidence that confuses our hearts?

The Word—Our Guide to Knowing God's Character

Trusting God is an essential part of growing spiritually strong. However, trust doesn't materialize out of nowhere—it comes as a result of knowing God's character and experiencing His presence in our lives. And where else, apart from the teaching of Scripture, can we find an accurate picture of who God is? Our knowledge can only begin with His revelation of himself.

Many great themes about God's character start in Genesis and flow through to Revelation. Three themes in particular point to why God can be trusted. Let's look at them.

God Is Sovereign

Nothing and no one has greater power than He has. He created and controls all that is. Speaking through Isaiah, God asserts, "From ancient days I am he. No one can deliver out of my hand. When I act, who can reverse it?" (43:13) Rebutting Pilate's claim to power over Him, Jesus said, "You would have no power over me if it were not given to you from above" (John 19:10-11).

In his book *Trusting God*, Jerry Bridges writes, "Because we know God is directing our lives to an ultimate end and because we know He is sovereignly able to orchestrate the events of our lives toward that end, we can trust Him. We can commit to Him not only the ultimate outcome of our lives but also all the intermediate events and circumstances that will bring us to that outcome."[3]

God Is All-Wise

He knows everything. He has all the facts. He sees and hears every motive, thought, and word. He promises that in all things (even those things that leave us utterly confused), He works for the good of those who love Him. Because He is all-wise, we're called to trust that what He gives or withholds is for our good. Yet because our understanding of God is imperfect, we often can't help but wonder, *How can this be true when it is so painful?*

God knows our struggles. He's tenderly aware of our human confusion and pain. Acknowledging our inability to understand His ways, He explains through Isaiah, "My thoughts are not your thoughts, neither are your ways my ways.... As the heavens are higher than the earth, so are my ways higher than your ways and my thoughts than your thoughts" (Isa. 55:8-9).

God Is Love

Because God is perfect, His love for us is perfect. Perfect love means no flaws, no imperfections, no cruelty, no callous indifference. If this is true, we can't accuse God of not loving us when life is painful and confusing. Neither can we say His love no longer exists or He's turned away from us for some unknown reason. Listen to Paul's words, then ask yourself, "When life hurts, does God still love me?"

"Who shall separate us from the love of Christ? Shall trouble or hardship or persecution or famine or nakedness or danger or sword? ... No, in all these things we are more than conquerors through Him who loved us.... Neither death nor life, neither angels nor demons, neither the present nor the future, nor any powers, neither height nor depth, nor anything else in all creation, will be able to separate us from the love of God that is in Christ Jesus our Lord" (Rom. 8:35-39).

Opportunities to trust happen more frequently than we'd like, but this is part of learning to walk with God. His goal is to develop our character and faith. To do this means bringing us, step by step, to the point in our lives where we can affirm, as Elisabeth Elliot did, that we believe and trust that God is sovereign, totally wise, and perfectly loving.

The circumstances God uses to develop this kind of trust will differ for each of us. Whatever form they take, look at every situation as His invitation to turn to the Word, search out His character, and learn to trust.

- Spend some moments thinking about a situation that confuses you. Write your thoughts as a question to God.

In what ways do the Scriptures regarding God's sovereignty, wisdom, and love help you?

Not long after Abraham started traveling through the land, he came face to face with various confusing circumstances. These were his opportunities to trust. Being human, and new to walking with God, however, his responses weren't always perfect—which I find encouraging.

The situations Abraham encountered were unique to him, but the spiritual lessons they contain apply to each of us, because growth is a maturing process for everyone. With this in mind, let's see what God wants us to learn when we're faced with confusing circumstances.

Confusing Circumstances Are Opportunities to Trust

We're not told how long it took Abraham and his household to travel to Shechem (Gen. 12:6-8). We are told, however, that the Canaanites were in the land. I wonder if this surprised Abraham. Was he confused? Had he assumed the land God told him to go to would be empty?

Imagine his situation. He'd trudged across hundreds of miles of desert, dragging his family away from relatives and friends, a comfortable life, and all that was familiar. He'd done what God asked—and now look what he found: other people living in what he considered his space. Exactly what was God up to? This very confusing new venture was not starting off as he'd expected.

Were those Abraham's thoughts? I don't know. I do know that's what I'd be thinking in similar circumstances.

Scripture doesn't tell us Abraham was confused by the Canaanites being in the land, or even if he was worried and anxious about their presence. We do know, however, that God knew exactly what he was thinking. Making His presence known at the exact time Abraham needed reassurance and encouragement, God affirmed His promise with the words "To your offspring I will give this land" (Gen. 12:7).

Expect God's Assurance and Encouragement

In the middle of Abraham's questions and confusion, God came to remind him to look up, not at his circumstances. He was not to worry or try to figure out how God would keep His promises. Abraham was to depend on God to do what He said, and to believe He would act in *His own time*. The land *was* going to be Abraham's. He *would* father a child. In fact, he'd have enough offspring to occupy the whole land—even though there was no sign of a baby on the way.

In confusing times, probably most of us yearn for God to assure and encourage us as He did Abraham. This does happen—if we have eyes to see.

Have you ever received a note or card when you were down in the dumps? Has someone called you at the precise moment you were crying and pleading with God to show you He loved you? Have you questioned your worth as a woman, a mother, or a wife, only to hear words of appreciation instead of feared criticism? It's as if God is audibly saying, "See, I'm still here. I know you're struggling, but you're my child. You're engraved on the palm of my hand. I haven't forgotten my promises to care for you."

Several years ago I went with Jim, my husband, on his six-month sabbatical from the hospital. The kids and I traveled with him to Kenya and London, which was a wonderful break. After being absent from teaching my Bible Study Fellowship class for a few months, however, I began to question whether they'd prefer my substitute to continue. The longer I was gone, the more I wondered if I should return.

Negative, discouraging thoughts flooded my mind. Maybe Sharon, my substitute, was much deeper, and was helping the class more than I could. Maybe the leaders preferred working with her. Could they be hoping I wouldn't come back and she would stay? By allowing the Enemy to come in like a flood and nearly drown me in doubt and confusion, I felt strongly tempted to resign and get it over with.

As the kids and I approached our apartment block one morning laden down with groceries, I felt both emotionally and physically worn out. Just then our daughter, Malaika, shouted, "Look, Mom, there's the mailman!" One of the letters was from a leader in my class. Her words shone with God's assurance, direction, and affirmation. He knew exactly what I was thinking and needing, a week before I did. He had prompted her to write seven days before, these words: "We are enjoying Sharon, but we miss you a lot. We're so looking forward to your coming back and being our teacher again."

- Knowing you are God's child, when have *you* experienced His assurance and encouragement? Recall the circumstances. How did God encourage you? What difference did this make in your heart?

If you're confused, feeling down, battling the Enemy's destructive words, take heart. Look up to Him, not at your circumstances. Watch for—and expect—His encouragement, remembering the words: "The Lord your God is with you.... He will take great delight in you, he will quiet you with his love, he will rejoice over you with singing" (Zeph. 3:17).

- Mull this over. Let God's love quiet your fears. Then take a moment to write down what you can confidently assert about your value to Him. Follow this by asking for some sign of His presence, some reassurance, some evidence of His care. Anticipate it, and be ready to rejoice when He answers.

Cultivating Worship Strengthens Our Ability to Trust

Abraham, in response to God's assurance, built an altar and worshiped "the Lord who had appeared to him." Moving on in this assurance, he built another altar near Bethel and called on the name of the Lord (Gen. 12:7-8). These two altars were the first of several that he built, demonstrating the key role worship played in his relationship with God. If we're going to walk with God, worship must become a regular part of our lives also.

But what, exactly, is worship—and why is it so important?

Worship Is ...?

Is worship the one-hour service you attend each week at your local church? Does worship happen only when you sing stirring praise songs, feel tingles and goose bumps, or raise your hands, clap, and cry? Or does worship happen any time we turn our attention to God, focusing on *His* character, *His* power, *His* deeds, and praising *Him* for who *He* is? In a later chapter we'll look more closely at the character of God. For now, let's consider what we mean by worship....

Scripture describes salvation as a free gift *received from* God. Worship, on the other hand, is shown as something presented *by us, to God* because He is utterly worthy of our adoration. Not all prayer or praise is worship. There's a difference:

Prayer brings needs *to God*: "Lord, help me," for example.

Praise relates to blessings *from God*: "I praise You, Lord, for helping me."

Worship focuses *on God* himself: "I adore You, Lord, for who You are."

Simply put, worship focuses on God's matchless worth—adoring Him, magnifying His name, and giving Him the glory He desires and deserves. This is wonderfully depicted in the fourth and fifth chapters of Revelation: "Holy, holy, holy is the Lord God Almighty, who was, and is, and is to come.... You are worthy, our Lord and God to receive glory and honor and power.... To him who sits on the throne and to the Lamb be praise and honor and glory and power, for ever and ever!" (Rev. 4:8, 11; 5:13).

Worship is not about us, but all about God. Worship is the creature's response of love to the Creator. The child's delight in her Father. The once shame-filled person's amazement at the mercy and forgiveness of a perfect God. Out of our gratitude and delight in Him, we long to honor and glorify the Father. God wants us to behold His glory and to give Him glory. We do this when we take time to worship.

In His wisdom, God has created us in such a way that as worship becomes part of our spiritual walk, we benefit. By focusing on His greatness and perfection, our ability to trust deepens. We also reap a spiritual vitality that permeates our lives with joy and peace.

Worship Produces Trust

Our awareness and appreciation of God deepens when we deliberately carve out time for worship. The result? A greater capacity to trust Him with the issues we face day by day.

Instead of worrying about our puny resources, worship reminds us that nothing is too hard for the Lord. He's the One who has unlimited power and divine resources beyond anything we can imagine. Knowing and believing these truths is how God enables us to rest rather than wrestle, to be anxious for nothing, and to experience peace even in the middle of hard times.

Most of us probably haven't arrived at perfect peace and rest in every situation, even though this is what God wants us to experience. He promises this is possible—but it won't happen unless we both practice and develop the habit of focusing on Him. Worship and trust are linked. Together they produce spiritual stability.

To cultivate the habit of worship takes deliberate effort. We don't grow in our knowledge and experience of who God is and how He acts, without spending time getting to know Him through reading and meditating on Scripture. "An unknown God can neither be trusted, served, nor worshiped," wrote Arthur W. Pink many years ago.[4] This truth hasn't changed—nor has the challenge it lays before us. Will we take time to know and worship our God? If you're wondering how or where to begin, consider these three suggestions:

- Buy yourself a notebook and reserve it specifically for spiritual reflection.

- Read slowly through the book of Isaiah, writing down verses and thoughts about God that nourish your heart. You could do the same with the book of Psalms—in fact, the whole of the Bible is a resource for spiritual enrichment, helping you to feel more comfortable learning to worship

God. Use the verses you've recorded as a springboard to worship, and then add your own thoughts of adoration as the Holy Spirit brings them to mind.

- Title separate pages in your notebook:

1. God's words—what He's said

2. God's works—what He's done

3. God's character—what He's like

4. Christ's work on the cross—what did He accomplish?

5. The Lord's present ministry in heaven

6. Christ's promised return

Look up verses about these subjects, writing down what you find in Scripture or from other sources. If you don't already have a concordance (a book that lists individual words in the Bible), buy or borrow one. This invaluable study aid will open your eyes to wonderful truths about God, starting you on a lifetime of praise.

When we neglect worship, we sentence ourselves to a shriveled view of God. Cultivate this vital part of walking with Him, and your concept of who He is and what He can do will continuously expand. So will your ability to trust Him.

- Because worship honors God and benefits the worshiper, consider the place it has in your spiritual journey. Jot down, as honestly as you can your reflections on worship and what role it currently has in your life.

- How would you like to see this area strengthened? What practical steps could you begin to take today to heighten your awareness and appreciation of God?

Crises of Faith Reveal Whom We Trust

"Now there was a famine in the land, and Abraham ..." (Gen. 12:10-20). What? Did he pray? Seek direction from the One who had appeared to him? Trust God to provide, based on His magnificent promises? No. In the face of crisis, Abraham panicked, forgot God, figured out his own solution, and headed off to Egypt.

After receiving God's assurance that he'd have an heir and possess the land—and even after building and worshiping at two altars—our man of faith flunks his first major test. Abraham was scared. His mind raced, thinking, *What am I to do? How am I supposed to survive?* Worry grabbed him by the throat—just as it does us when the unexpected happens.

I'm sure Abraham thought, *God, what are you doing? You told me I'd be blessed by coming here. I obeyed you and thought you'd take care of our needs. What is going on? Don't you care, after all?*

Difficult situations don't necessarily mean we're out of God's will. His goal is to develop our faith. To do this, He will sometimes allow a famine to touch our lives, as He did with Abraham.

Famine—A God-Permitted Time of Need

A famine, as we've so frequently seen in Africa, is a time of severe need. Abraham faced a physical famine, but there are many other kinds. Whenever you face a situation you're powerless to do anything about, you're in a famine.

Perhaps you can say as Abraham did, "There's a famine in my life": a job layoff or a big problem at work, a family or church conflict, a frightening diagnosis or chronic illness, a painful loss, a longing for friends or connection or purpose in life. You're drying up inside for lack of life and soul-sustaining nourishment. You thirst for peace or love or acceptance. And like Abraham you wonder, *God, why? What are you doing?*

Moving to Singapore with my husband a few years ago, I experienced my own severe famine—of friendship, connection, ministry, and daily purpose. Everything that had been a normal part of my life was gone. I knew no one in the country, and no one knew me. The famine didn't pass quickly—they usually don't. Yet I firmly believed we were in God's will. Because of that conviction, I clung to what I knew about God—but that didn't stop me from feeling lonely and miserable for a few months. After all, God made us with emotions. He doesn't ask us to ignore or deny our feelings. He invites us to cling to Him in spite of them.

Famines can be physical and tangible needs such as money, a place to live, or a job; or they might be emotional or spiritual. Whatever form they take, God uses them—not to punish, but to push us forward. He didn't cause the famine, but He allowed it in order to develop Abraham's trust—and He permits them in our lives for the same reason.

In addition to deepening our trust, a famine reminds us of how much we need God day by day. Remember the prayer Jesus taught: "Give us *this day* our daily bread"? Without periodic famines of one kind or another, it's so easy to forget our need of God and live as if He is unnecessary. Given the pressure of our fallen nature and our culture to be independent, proactive, and self-sufficient, this is a very real danger. What a contrast to the humble dependency we see modeled by the Lord that is supposed to characterize our lives. It's only when famine strikes that we relearn something so easily forgotten: God alone can provide for our deepest needs.

In the Grip of Worry

Few of us go through life without confronting some seemingly real fears: How can we stretch our income to cover the bills? Is my marriage going to survive—or will I become a single mom? What will the doctor tell me at the next appointment? What kinds of choices will our kids make—and how can I cope with the choices they've already made? How can I help my ailing parents? How can the fractures and conflict in our family be healed?

When our minds lock on to these kinds of fears, what happens? Do we feel joy, peace, and trust in God? Hardly. Caught in the grip of worry, don't we often react like Abraham did, forgetting God and figuring out our own solutions?

Worry is the termite of the soul, tunneling its way into the very support beams of our lives. Taking over our thoughts, it eats away at our trust in God, step by step. Let's use Abraham's experience in Genesis 12:10-20 to trace the downward spiral worry kicks off.

As a Result of Worry, We Can ...

- **Forget God.** Crisis is an opportunity to *remember* God's promises and to develop faith muscles. Facing a famine, Abraham reacted as if God's promises didn't exist. Spiritually, he blanked out. He didn't seek divine help. He could have said to himself, "Wait a minute. God told me this was my land and that I will have offspring."

  Thinking logically, he could have further reasoned, "I am not going to die—God is going to provide, even though I have no idea how."

- **Lose Faith.** Forget about God, and faith doesn't have a chance to lift your perspective from panic to trust. Like helium leaking out of a balloon, as soon as Abraham forgot God; his faith fizzled down to nothing.

- **Experience Fear.** By leaving God out of the picture, fear takes over. Add a fertile imagination, and Abraham could see his household and all his animals slowly starving to death. What else could they expect? When a famine hits, you can't sit around waiting for God to do something unheard of like calling ravens to fly in food or to drop manna from the sky ... could you?

- **Feel Insecure.** Fear breeds insecurity. "What's going to happen? How will I survive? What if this means?" Insecurity breeds pressure to act. "I have to do something, anything. I can't just sit around waiting for God to act, I've got to make decisions NOW." Thoughts of waiting on God for His wisdom fly out the window. Too often we act impulsively because of the emotional pressure bearing down on us. Then, like Abraham, we find we've jumped from the frying pan into the fire.

- **Behave Selfishly.** Panic and insecurity crowd out everything but self-preservation. Arriving on Egypt's border, Abraham suddenly thought, *Uh oh. Now what am I going to do? Sarah is so beautiful, the Egyptian king will want to take her. That will mean curtains for me. I've got to figure this out. Wait a minute—if we just bend the truth a little, tell them she's my half-sister, then I'll be fine. They'll treat me well and my life will be spared.*

Notice: No thought is given to Sarah's feelings or safety. For Abraham, it's all "What about ME? How will I get out of this?" When the flesh is in control, selfishness crowds into the driver's seat. Instead of protecting Sarah as his wife and the mother of his promised heir, he was ready to sacrifice her for his own safety!

- **Act Hypocritically.** Where is our true character best seen? Someone has said, "Character is what we are in the dark." It's also true to say, "Character is who we are under pressure." Abraham was admired by his household as a man who knew and worshiped the one true God. They looked to him as their spiritual leader, thinking he trusted God.

  Your own need to grow in trust is often hidden until we're under pressure—but don't be discouraged. Even though Abraham's faith didn't go as deep as the situation demanded, God was at work.

- **Receive a Rebuke.** If we neglect to seek God's direction, as Abraham did, He doesn't necessarily stop us from going our own way. Nor does He always shield us from the consequences of our actions. Receiving a sharp rebuke or scornful comment can be a painful reminder to turn to God early on the next time.

The Lord did rescue both Sarah and Abraham from Abraham's folly by inflicting a plague on Pharaoh's household. Needless to say, Pharaoh wasn't too happy about this. Confronting an ashamed man of faith, Pharaoh angrily told Abraham to take his wife and get going. So much for being a blessing.

The Unseen Battle

When we don't trust God under pressure, testings, and difficulties, we spiral downward like Abraham did. It's as if we've entered a spiritual war zone blindfolded. Too often, we're not even aware that a battle is raging—a battle for victory in our lives. God's desire is to use whatever troubles us to draw us closer to himself. At the same time, Satan, our spiritual enemy, wants to trip us up, ensnare, and devour us (2 Tim. 2:26; Eph. 6:10-13).

Confusing, worrisome circumstances always confront us with spiritual choices. Can I trust God? Will He come through for me? Could I possibly do what I sense He is asking of me? We wrestle with these issues, getting our eyes off God and onto ourselves. Battling fears and doubts without God's help, you might be sinking right now under the taunts of the Enemy.

At times the battle to trust can be exhausting and seem never-ending—but it must be fought, often over and over again. Jesus spoke of our common struggle with fear in Matthew 6:25-34. He referred five times to worry—not meaning those times when you have to mull over decisions, but the fear-building, wearying worry that consumes your peace, devouring both emotional and spiritual energy.

"Don't worry," Jesus commands—and He gives two solid reasons why:

1. You have a heavenly Father who loves and values you. He will provide for you (v. 26).

2. Worry cannot change your circumstances (v. 27).

God can change our circumstances if it's His will, but worry can't. What it can do, however, is make us emotionally and physically ill. Thinking that expressing worry for someone shows how much we love him, we proudly call ourselves a worrywart. We say to family and friends, "I just can't help it, I care about her so much." But the blunt truth is worry amounts to disobedience, which is a sin. Oops. This is a tough truth, right?

Equating worry with sin isn't something most of us like. When Jesus speaks against greed, hypocrisy, or immorality, we take His words seriously—but worry? That's normal—just part of being human. How can you really care for someone, the argument goes, if you don't worry about that person when he or she faces tough times? But ask yourself: What does my worry reveal? That I trust God? That He is able to work in the situation that concerns me? That He loves me and will sustain me and my loved one who is facing tough times?

Learning to trust and not worry is as much a growing place as learning to control our tongue or our temper. In encouraging our growth, God doesn't merely tell us what to do, He shows us how to make this a reality in our lives. In chapter 4 of Philippians, Paul gives us clear instructions: Figure out what's worrying you. Tell God *all* about it. Make your requests known, and thank Him for His power to provide what's needed (vv. 6-7).

In every spiritual struggle, we're not just wrestling with our old habit patterns or personality type, we're fighting an unseen Enemy. Whispering words of hopelessness and fear, Satan wants to induce panic and despair when we encounter pressures, testings, and difficulties. God's goal is to produce spiritual growth and strength. This is the unseen—and often, unrealized—battle for our faith.

As you reflect on your own inner battles, look at the contrasting outcomes. Then ask yourself: Which is happening in *my* life?

Two Outcomes from Pressures, Testings, and Difficulties

Satan Tempts Me to:	God Desires Me to:
Focus on:	*Focus on:*
My suffering, my need	His sufficiency, His strength
Satan's Objective:	*God's Objective*
To drag me away from God	To draw me closer to Him
Natural Choice:	*Godly Choice:*
Self-pity	To receive strength
Bitterness	Bear fruit
Cynicism	Deepen my trust
Hopelessness/fear	Have hope and joy

When you're tempted to fall into worry and despair, think about who God is, believe everything good you know of Him—and keep bringing your thoughts back to Him whenever they wander. Do this over and over and you'll train your mind to trust—not worry.

The Path to Trust

Speaking to Abraham's descendents, the prophet Jeremiah called out, "Stand at the crossroads and look; ask for the ancient paths, ask where the good way is, and walk in it, and you will find rest for your souls" (Jer. 6:16). Crises are crossroads—those places where decisions are made and consequences are set in motion.

In contrast to the downward spiral worry produces, Jeremiah points to God's solution. In times of confusion and worry, Jeremiah says, *Spiral upward* by choosing to stand, look, ask, walk, and rest.

- **Stand:** When life is scary—quietly stand still with a sense of expectation. Affirm your belief that the Lord brought you to this place—it is not by accident. He has led you this far and He will continue to lead you through and beyond what you are facing today.

- **Look:** This includes pondering, thinking, and weighing what's before you in the light of God's character and promises. Think about your options and the likely results of each one—not only now but also down the road. Consider not only yourself but also others who will be affected. When you're tempted to act in panic, remember Abraham.

- **Ask:** Give yourself time to pray, seek wisdom, and wait for God to work. Recall those principles God has provided for the kind of situation you're facing. Then give it all to Him; trust Him to take you through it; depend on Him to act on your behalf.

- **Walk:** After asking God to provide what you need, walk forward in the confidence He will give. Echo the truth Paul gave to Timothy over and over in your heart: "God did not give us a spirit of timidity, but a spirit of power, of love and of self-discipline" (2 Tim. 1:7). This really works.

- **Rest:** God promises rest—the absence of panic and hopelessness—when we rely on Him to guide us in our times of confusion. Jesus also promised rest when we come to Him. God wants us to have supernatural inner peace and a quiet spirit. He longs for us to trust that we *are* under His watchful care. In this way, we not only experience His tender assurance, we live it, and have something real to share with a confused and needy world.

Daily Choices for the Growing Heart
Trust God in Confusing Circumstances

I know what a struggle it is to cast off fear and trust God.

I also know that we don't have to allow our minds to act like a trap, holding us in the grip of anxiety and dread. This is never what God wants—and I'm sure you don't, either.

To enjoy God's peace when you find yourself in scary situations:

- View feelings of fear or thoughts of hopelessness as signals to turn to God.

- Use confusion and crisis to remind you that God is sovereign, loving, and a steadying help in time of trouble.

- Spiral upward by fixing your mind on God's power, not your powerlessness.

- Strengthen yourself with the psalmist's words: "When I am afraid, I WILL trust in you."

Six

Consider Conflict as an Opportunity to Grow

Assuming the worst about the intentions of others only brings trouble.[1]

𝒥alking to her nine-year-old son early one morning, Florence asked, "How are things going with you this morning?" With a big sigh, Freddie replied, "Pretty good so far, Mom—I haven't run into any people yet."[2]

Freddie sounded wise for his age. Maybe he'd tangled with other kids in his neighborhood or been bullied at school. Whatever he'd personally experienced, Freddie understood a gritty fact of human relationships. When people rub shoulders with people, conflicts happen.

Everywhere we turn we find trouble: marriage conflicts, family clashes, hurtful friends, difficult bosses or co-workers, church disagreements, domineering committee or small group members, or obnoxious neighbors. Sometimes it seems life would be much easier if other people weren't around to mess up our moods, object to our plans, or disagree with our opinions. The problem is, keeping away from the rest of humanity isn't God's answer to avoiding or preventing conflict.

You and I are supposed to be involved in relationships, even if some people tick you off, irritate, annoy, infuriate, or make you grind your teeth. Our call is to penetrate the world with Christ's love, be part of the church, care for our neighbor, work, build understanding, and willingly serve others. That doesn't happen if we hide in our caves, coming out only when we absolutely have to.

If you want to fulfill God's purposes but dread the thought of dealing with prickly people and sticky situations, what can you do? Just hope and pray that everyone likes you? That you will like them? Avoid ever having a difference of opinion with anyone? Play that game, and maybe you'll avoid conflict—but I doubt it.

Strife happens even when you do your best to avoid it: say your teen wants to spend spring break driving your car cross-country—by herself; or your mother complains you're neglecting her because you don't call every day; then your neighbor lops off half the branches of your favorite tree because it slightly leans over on his side of the fence. It's enough to make any sensible person mutter, "Good grief, what's the matter with people? Why can't they be as reasonable and easygoing as I am?"

Too often discord and misunderstanding provoke even stronger emotions.

"I don't want to attend my son's wedding," my friend Pam announced. Tears streamed down her face as she angrily described her future daughter-in-law's behavior: "She didn't invite me to the bridal shower. She won't let any of our family join them for opening their wedding gifts, yet she's invited *her* family." I gave her a comforting hug, knowing that was all I could do. Another friend, Betty, confided her hurt feelings. "I couldn't believe how a close friend treated me this week," she said. "Three of us often get together for lunch—but when I told Tammy I couldn't join her and Natalie that day, she joked, 'Oh, then we can talk about you because you won't be there.'

"I said, 'No, no, I don't want you to do that,' but she responded that they could do what they wanted."

Both Pam and Betty were hurt, shocked, and angry. We've all been there at some time or other. We're human, we have feelings, and we all react one way or another to conflict. You might react differently than I would. Your spouse or friend might react differently than you. Whatever your style of response to difficult people and situations, knowing how you react is an important step toward personal and spiritual growth.

My Natural Reaction Is ...

Our natural response to conflict is like our natural response to anything—our sinful nature jumps into action and reveals itself one way or another. Bitten by the sin bug, we're often too quick to blame others and defend ourselves. Adam began the first marital battle by doing exactly this. When God asked why he and Eve were suddenly hiding behind bushes, Adam defended himself by promptly blaming Eve—and, of course, God as well (Gen. 3).

Depending on your personal style, when you're having a run-in with someone, you might get coldly furious or spitting mad. Cain was the spitting-mad type. His resentment against his brother, Abel, went from simmer to boil before spilling over into murder. Saul allowed cold fury and jealousy to eat him up. Determined to be rid of his rival,

David, he relentlessly sought David's destruction. In the end, his ugly obsession destroyed him (Gen. 4; 1 Sam. 18-31).

Each of us has our own way of responding to prickly people or sticky situations.

If you watched your father sulk and hold grudges, or your mother blow her top and rant against someone she disagreed with, you might do the same—even though you vowed you'd be different. Maybe you fought to be heard in your family, so you learned to be a scrapper—or your only sense of safety lay in pleasing the one who had power over you.

Multiple reasons exist for why we handle differences the way we do—family modeling, genes, personality, hormones. Even though our reactions vary, however, there are some common styles of responding to conflict. Consider these four:

- **Cathy Controller:** Believes she knows best. Competes for control. Wants decisions to go her way and will fight as long as necessary to achieve her goal. Frequently refuses to accept personal responsibility for the conflict.

- **Mary Manipulator:** Operates behind the scenes— passing on information, stirring up issues, making judgmental comments without checking her facts.

- **Annie Avoider:** Very uncomfortable differing openly with others—but not happy with what is happening. Avoids conflict, but harbors grudges. Erects silent, invisible walls and is unwilling to initiate reconciliation.

- **Christy Capitulator:** Gives in either because she doesn't feel strongly about an issue or is unwilling to stand up for the greater good. Accommodating, but often feels taken advantage of.

Did you recognize yourself a teensy bit in one or more of these examples? Unfortunately, I did. Even so, let's take heart. Growth doesn't come from denying or dodging the truth, but from admitting it and asking the Lord to make us more like Him. Be brave—and take another step toward knowing yourself by answering the following questions.

- Describe your way of responding to prickly people or sticky situations. What do you usually do or say? How do you feel about them? About your own response?

- How do you usually resolve conflicts?

- What changes, if any, would you like to see in your responses?

I Can't Help My Reaction ... Can I?

The Bible is full of stories about people who found themselves in every kind of human conflict. Like us, each of them faced a choice. Adam could have taken personal responsibility. Cain could have asked God for help to deal with his anger. Saul could have repented of his jealousy and sin. All three looked at their situations through the grid of their attitudes. This, in turn, drove their actions.

Once they allowed sinful feelings and attitudes to take control, their lives were changed forever. Others also were greatly harmed by their evil choices. In conflicts, as in other areas of life, the law of sowing and reaping affects many.

Whether minor or major, conflicts present us with choices. We can accept them as God-permitted opportunities to grow more like Christ, or we can let them shrivel our souls. Much as we'd rather not have our feelings hurt and be on the receiving end of unfair treatment without protest, these experiences actually can draw us closer to the Lord. In the middle of conflicts, we have to trust our reputations to God, let go of the rights we feel entitled to, and accept the good or bad outcome of relationships. Most important, the Spirit uses these times to teach us about ourselves, our need for humility, and the value of being as sensitive to the rights of others as we are to our own.

With Christ, Change Is Possible

Jesus' power is available to refine the way we handle these spiritually and emotionally tough situations. Paul states, "You, however, are controlled not by the sinful nature but by the Spirit, if the Spirit of God lives in you" (Rom. 8:9). Satan doesn't want us to believe this. Neither can he stand for us to release our grudges, turning strife and division into a glorious testimony to what God can do in the human heart.

Peter understood this when he wrote, "Dear friends, I urge you, as aliens and strangers in the world, to abstain from sinful desires, which war against your soul" (1 Pet. 2:11). Pastor and author Stuart Briscoe comments that the war against the soul "refers to the things that go on within the inner recesses of a human being's personality that can lead to the destruction of what that person is intended to be.... If we don't handle these things properly, an individual can be rendered spiritually impotent."[3]

Consider what these Scriptures teach: Even though you normally react to conflict by chewing over slights and stewing in bitterness, you're not chained to that response. Maybe you stuff your feelings and keep smiling for the sake of harmony, but you can find healthier ways to resolve differences. Because "the Spirit of God lives in you," He enables you to "abstain from sinful desires" by changing your perspective, your attitude, and your actions.

Listen to God's Spirit: You're not a robot programmed to react with sinful attitudes. You don't have to respond as you might have done in the past, missing what God wants to do in and through you today. You don't have to go on being spiritually impotent. You have a choice.

Satan, the essence of selfishness, wants to do what he's always done: confuse your mind, cripple your spiritual effectiveness, and bring conflict between you and others. God's aim is the opposite. Filling your mind with His truth, empowering you with His Spirit, and calling you to His unity, He wants conflict to be used for your growth, His glory, and the good of others.

Scripture is full of wisdom about handling difficult situations. We're also given true-to-life examples to learn from. Abraham's wise and generous response to Lot and the fight between their herdsmen reveals attitudes and actions that have much to teach us today. Before we look at those lessons, however, let's explore why he was able to respond in the way he did.

To Grow Through Conflict:

Stay Close to God

Our last glimpse of Abraham showed him trudging out of Egypt, no doubt struggling with guilt and feeling thoroughly ashamed of himself. Then something happened between that near-disaster and his gracious faith-filled response to the quarrel between his herdsmen and Lot's. The record tells us: "He went from place to place until he came to Bethel ... where he had first built an altar. There Abraham called on the name of the Lord" (Gen. 13:3-4).

Here's our first clue to what lay behind his godly attitude. He gave priority to restoring his damaged fellowship with God.

Get Right With God

When Abraham messed up in Egypt, he knew it. Loving God as he did, he must have been appalled by what he'd done. Why didn't he go straight back to Bethel? We don't know. Was he trying to avoid God? Was he struggling with a guilty conscience, as all humans so often do? Perhaps.

Without any clear instructions to guide him, Abraham nevertheless sensed the Spirit drawing him back to Bethel. Arriving there, he called on the name of the Lord, once again submitting his heart and life to God.

Abraham didn't justify his actions or make excuses for what he'd done. His faith had faltered, he'd taken his eyes off God, and he'd grown cold. He knew this all too well. But having tasted the thrill of walking with God, he yearned for that same closeness once again. He couldn't settle for a broken-down, dried-up faith. He longed for a return to that intense closeness with God.

What God taught Abraham, He wants to teach us: When our eyes turn away from Him and onto ourselves, our faith shrivels up. Instead of consciously trusting Him, we depend on our own strengths and resources. Before we know it, we mess up as Abraham did. Ever done this? Ever felt guilty, and sorry about failing God, and wandered around avoiding Him? I have. Coming back to Bethel—the House of Bread, the place of spiritual nourishment and strength—is the only answer to our dryness and the sin that inevitably follows.

To get right with God, refuse to stay away from Him. Open the door of your heart, asking Him to do what only He can. Believe that in His love He will forgive, wipe away your guilt and sorrow, and bestow on you "a crown of beauty instead of ashes, the oil of gladness instead of mourning, and a garment of praise instead of a spirit of despair" (Isa. 61:3). Taking these steps to get right with God brings back the joy of our salvation—and enables us to have God-given strength when grappling with difficult relationships.

A second vital ingredient for growth is a refocused mind.

Refocus Your Mind

Restoring his relationship with God changed Abraham's distorted perspective. Instead of thinking he had to depend on himself and figure out his own solutions, coming back into God's presence had refocused his mind on who was really in control.

He no longer had to worry about his life or possessions, and he didn't have to figure out what to do next. He was directed and protected by the One who had called him years before when he lived in Ur. Even his overlong stay in Haran hadn't prevented this same God from forgiving and calling him again.

God had given him divine promises of a family and a land for them to dwell in. In addition, God promised he'd be blessed and be a blessing. Reflecting on all of these incredible promises, Abraham's heart must have overflowed with assurance and gratitude. He could see that his future lay in God's hands. Scheming, manipulating, and clinging to his rights was not necessary—God would take care of him.

Because he'd refocused his mind on God's power and His plans for his life, Abraham's ability to trust God became strong and steady. Even though he didn't know what lay ahead, he was spiritually prepared.

- If a conflict erupted in your life today, how do you think you'd respond? In the flesh, or in faith? What makes you think this?

- What biblical truths come to mind about God's loving purposes for you? Jot down two or three. How can focusing on these give you inner assurance when facing difficult people or unfair situations?

Shoving, Shouting, and Solving Problems

Abraham's wealth increased greatly as a result of his impulsive escapade in Egypt. Instead of having stocks and shares in a bull market, his prosperity was in actual bulls, cows, sheep, and servants. These had been his payoff for allowing Pharaoh to take Sarah into his harem.

Unknowingly, Pharaoh's generosity laid the groundwork for the coming separation between Abraham and Lot. God's will that Abraham leave his father's household was going to happen. And

He used Abraham's folly and Pharaoh's finances to bring it about (Gen. 13).

Back in Canaan, the herds of livestock belonging to both men kept increasing. So did their competing needs for grazing land and access to water. In their determination to take care of the herds entrusted to them, Lot's and Abraham's servants soon began shoving, shouting, and slinging insults at each other. The situation threatened to escalate into a free-for-all.

When Abraham and Lot found themselves caught in this feud, Abraham, as head of the family, could have thrown his weight around. He had every right to put Lot in his place, declaring in no uncertain terms who was boss. Instead, his trust in God enabled him to handle the situation in such a way that good rather than harm resulted.

Assessing the situation, Abraham could see they needed to part company. He invited Lot to choose where he wanted to go. Lot looked up, hardly believing his good fortune, and opted for the best available land. Abraham didn't protest, accuse him of incredible selfishness, or say "good riddance." Graciously, he let Lot take what he wanted. Even though they parted company, Abraham was determined there would be no rift between them. How often does this happen?

Because Abraham's heart had been restored and refocused on God, his attitude and actions contain lessons for us. Long before the New Testament instructed us to live in peace as much as possible, esteem others above ourselves, and preserve unity, Abraham practiced these principles. He also practiced forgiveness, refusing to carry a grudge against Lot in spite of his self-centered and pushy behavior.

In the face of squabbling and power-hungry tactics, Abraham responded with gracious attitudes and wise words. Hard as it is, this is exactly the kind of stunning reaction God wants to develop in us. Abraham may have failed in Egypt, but he shines in this incident.

Isn't it encouraging to see his growth—and doesn't it give you hope for your own?

To grow through conflict, we should approach each touchy situation in the Spirit rather than in the flesh. Abraham's response is a God-given example of this. Let's look at three principles he models that allow God to bring good out of what is potentially mean and selfish.

- Anticipate a positive outcome.
- Aim to preserve relationships.
- Apply good communication skills.

Anticipate a Positive Outcome

Clearly, Abraham believed a positive outcome to a legitimate problem was possible. So did Cheryl, whose feelings had been deeply hurt by her friend Donna's critical comments about Molly, her daughter. Cheryl struggled with what to do. She valued her friendship with Donna and dreaded the possibility of damaging it, but ...

After praying about the situation for a few weeks, Cheryl knew that unless she talked frankly to Donna, this issue would drive a wedge between them. Either way, their friendship was at stake.

Knocking on her friend's door, Cheryl mentally rehearsed what she would say when Donna appeared. She didn't have long to wait. "Donna," she burst out, as soon as the door opened, "I want to talk to you about something that's been bothering me. May I come in?"

After telling Donna how she felt, Cheryl listened, shocked, as Donna responded that her feelings had been hurt on various occasions, as well, by things Cheryl had said. Rather than bristling with indignation and arguing over who was at fault, Cheryl apologized. "Can we forgive each other and remain friends?" she asked. After tears, apologies, and hugs, they both realized with joy that God had helped them deal with their differences.

Can conflict be used by God to build relationships? Absolutely. He can bring good out of evil, give us strength where we're weak, and provide courage when we're gripped by fear. If He's able to do these marvelous things, can't He also heal the rifts that so easily divide us from one another? Of course He can. But we have to cooperate. We must go to the person, resist an accusing attitude, and look for the good God can bring out of conflict.

Go to the Person

Abraham didn't avoid discussing the problem he and Lot faced, and neither did Cheryl. Both of them did what Jesus taught: Go to the person you're in conflict with and *confront* him or her (Matt. 5:23-24; 18:15-17).

Now, before you think this means blaming, accusing, or picking a fight, understand what *confrontation* means. The *New American College Dictionary* describes it: "To stand or come in front of; stand or meet facing.... To bring together for examination or comparison." In contrast, the same dictionary says *conflict* is "to come into a collision, clash, or to be in opposition or at variance. To contend; do battle."

Confrontation and conflict are two radically different ways to handle problems. One is healthy and has the goal of building relationships, the other too often becomes an excuse to attack, tear down, and emerge the winner.

In his helpful book, *Confronting Without Guilt or Conflict*, Bob Weyant echoes Jesus' teaching. To keep a problem from escalating into outright conflict, he recommends: "Go to the person immediately, in private, with respect, and request a change of behavior and come to some resolution."[4]

If you can't let go of an issue and move on, ask yourself if God is leading you to deal with it by confronting (coming in front of) the other party, calmly and respectfully. I'll be the first to admit this sounds intimidating. Even though Jesus told us to do this, promising His grace and help, we still shrink from what He said for fear of being verbally attacked or making the situation worse. But what happens when we don't "come in front of" with the desire to resolve differences respectfully? Don't we, instead, usually avoid the person who hurt or offended us? And doesn't this gradually build a wall between us and cause the relationship to cool?

Wanting to do what was right and possibly save their friendship, Cheryl did what Jesus tells us to do. She prepared to come in front of Donna by praying for wisdom and courage. At the same time she confessed her sinful attitudes, she also asked God to work in Donna, helping her to be open and responsive. Cheryl believed He would do His part, but she also had to do hers if she hoped to see a positive outcome. Avoidance would not bring resolution.

Resist Responding From Your Old Nature

Much as we wish all conflicts would end with both sides wanting to rebuild the relationship, the fact is they don't. Just because you're full of the Spirit and want a positive outcome doesn't guarantee the other person shares your attitude. If despite your best efforts to discuss the problem calmly the other person verbally attacks, resist the temptation to respond in kind. Excuse yourself and leave it for a better time.

Describing recent events in her church, Charlotte commented, "Even though the leaders of our church called a public meeting and tried to explain why the pastor left, some people were so angry they made wild accusations against them. It broke my heart to see these good Christian men treated like this. Their ability to give calm and loving answers was proof of their desire to respond in a way that pleased the Lord."

Hurtful encounters, whether in the church, workplace, family, or a friendship, damage our sense of security. Our trust in a particular person or group of people can easily be shattered, leaving us disillusioned and battling bitterness. We shrink from standing up to the domineering man or woman who heedlessly criticizes and tears down whomever differs with them. Silenced by those powerful personalities, many timidly swallow their objections and say nothing. As a result, "might" too often conquers "right."

When clashes between Christians become public, they do even greater damage. These divisions hinder prayer, weaken younger believers, offend the Holy Spirit, and earn the scorn of non-believers. They also give Satan a foothold to incite grudges, gossip, and division.

Responding to differences from our old human nature is never pleasing to God. Scripture repeatedly commands Christians not to slander anyone, but rather to treat others with consideration, making every effort to resolve conflicts peaceably (Tit. 3:1-2). This applies even to those who have mistreated us. Abraham modeled this response. So did Cheryl when her friendship with Donna stood in jeopardy. What response do others see from you or me?

Look for the Positive

Can hurtful encounters ever be beneficial? Surprisingly, the answer is yes. Approached with prayer and responded to in God's power, confrontation and even conflict can have positive results. Consider these encouraging facts:

1. Conflict can help communication be more honest. Instead of burying irritations or hurts, conflict gives the opportunity to speak the truth *in love*.

2. Conflict can clarify goals. Do you know what you want? Do you know what the other person wants? What do you need from each other? Conflict forces you to think clearly, define your goals, and listen to the other person with respect.

3. Conflict can bring about mutual understanding between people, couples, or a team. By listening to others and paying attention to their feelings, you increase your ability to understand why they reacted as they did.

4. Conflict can clear the air, making way for a fresh beginning. When differences are discussed calmly and objectively, the Holy Spirit can produce a new respect and relationship that honors Him.

5. Conflict can reveal new solutions to old problems. Unresolved issues can hang over relationships like shadowy cobwebs. Each party knows they're there, but no one wants to sweep them down. During a conflict, however, their existence can be acknowledged and fresh solutions sought.

Cheryl had been offended and hurt by Donna's words, but she believed a positive outcome was possible. Counting on God's promise to instruct and teach her in the way she should go, Cheryl trusted Him to show her how to approach Donna. "It was scary," she admitted, "but I'm glad I went. God wonderfully answered my prayers. Now Donna and I are closer than ever."

Be encouraged—a positive outcome is possible. And even if it doesn't turn out exactly as you'd hoped, you'll have grown by trusting and obeying what Jesus asks you to do.

- As you reflect on a sticky situation you've experienced, what part did you find most difficult? Did you go to the person? Resist reacting in your old nature? Find some positive outcome?

- What helpful lessons have you learned from experiencing conflict?

Aim to Preserve Relationships

When Abraham learned of the fighting between their herdsmen, he responded to Lot, "Let's not have any quarreling between you and me ... for we are brothers." Even though he was head of the household, Abraham treasured his relationship with Lot. Maintaining unity was a higher priority to him than asserting his power or preferences. What a difference it would make if we responded like Abraham when other believers ruffle our feathers.

Preserving relationships takes effort when your confidence has been betrayed, your feelings are hurt, or your cherished beliefs are attacked. Nevertheless, it's possible—if we value what Jesus values: unity of heart, acceptance of others, and a humble attitude.

Work Toward Unity, Not Uniformity of Convictions

With His crucifixion imminent, the issue of unity weighed on Jesus' heart. He prayed that all who follow Him would be one, just as He and the Father are one. Echoing the Lord, Paul urged

Christians to make every effort to keep the unity of the Spirit (John 17:11; Eph. 4:3).

No matter how we differ with other believers on various issues—raising or not raising hands in worship, women in leadership roles, modes of baptism, speaking in tongues, or hymns versus praise songs—God wants us to place high value on the fact that we are, first of all, *brothers and sisters.*

"My daughter's husband is from another church background," Alexis confided. "I don't agree with some of his beliefs, but I'm careful not to say anything. He loves the Lord, so I keep reminding myself we're all one in Christ and that's what really matters."

Rather than debating different interpretations of certain Scriptures, Alexis works to maintain unity of heart with her son-in-law, Jeff. Fortunately for everyone involved, she doesn't feel the need to argue and force him over to her view. When the issues aren't of primary importance, Alexis would rather keep harmony than build tension.

No matter how strongly we hold certain doctrines, we'll know the full truth only when we're in heaven. What we do know now, however, is that God loves and accepts *all* who have put their faith in Christ. No one group of Christians has a monopoly on His love and favor—or an inside track on what He really meant by some passages.

Accept Those Who Differ From You

Considering our diverse upbringings, cultures, ages, and spiritual experiences, different views on secondary issues are to be expected. To call ourselves Christians, of course, we must hold as true those essential doctrines that proclaim the uniqueness of our faith. Some of these are the message of the Cross, the divinity of Christ, and salvation through faith in Him alone. Beyond unity on the essentials, however, God's goal is not rigid uniformity of thought on everything from the earth's beginnings to the end times.

Our Creator, who made us distinct from one another, doesn't expect us to agree on every issue—but He does expect us to live in peace and unity with other members of the body. "The body is a unit, though it is made up of many parts; and though all its parts are many, they form one body. So it is with Christ. For we were all baptized by one Spirit into one body—whether Jews or Greeks, slave or free— and we were all given the one Spirit to drink" (1 Cor. 12:12-13).

Choose a Humble Attitude

Although humility isn't highly valued in our culture, it is highly valued by God. Paul points to Christ as our supreme example: "Being found in appearance as a man, he humbled himself and became obedient to death—even death on a cross!" (Phil. 2:8). Humility and love released the healing power of the cross, which is also released when we choose to handle conflicts in a spirit of humility and love.

To be humble doesn't mean being a doormat. Jesus could never be seen in that light. No, coming from an inner core of strength rather than weakness, humility is a voluntary choice to "bow down and make low."

What does humility look like in practical terms when tempers explode or people are seething at work, in your neighborhood, or at church? How about deliberately choosing to restrain yourself—to not argumentatively push your agenda or stir up people to take your side? What about considering how the other party thinks or feels? You could also adopt a Christlike response that says, "I'm going to listen carefully and try to understand where they are coming from. Even more, I want us to come to an agreement on what the problem is and find a fair solution to our differences."

Start modeling humility when the sparks are flying, and you'll end up a peacemaker—which is exactly what Jesus calls us to be.

Apply Good Communication Skills

With his heart restored and his mind refocused on God, Abraham was spiritually ready to deal with the conflict in his household. This becomes evident in his willingness to listen and consider what solution would work best for all involved.

Would you like to know if you're spiritually ready to deal with conflict? To tell whether you're under the control of the Spirit or your own will? Here's a surefire test: The Spirit softens our hearts, moving us to listen and hear the other person's point of view. When our own wills are in control, our hearts grow hard, poisoned by dislike, distrust, and a determination not to give an inch.

Because conflict is a God-permitted opportunity to grow spiritually, let's assume you do desire to understand the other person and resolve your problem. What should you do?

Your heart is right with God. You've confessed your own faults. You're willing to go and talk to the person. But what will you say? How do you approach him or her? Here are some suggestions:

- Don't assume the worst about the other person. We instinctively think he is the enemy wanting to harm our reputation or us. Calm down—this is usually not the case.

- Invite her to talk about the problem between you. Choose a private place and allow plenty of time for a productive conversation. Having your kids in tow, an appointment within the hour, or meeting in a crowded restaurant only adds stress.

- Remember, perception and reality are often confused. You may think something about the situation that is totally different from the other person's understanding. Build respect and trust by asking to hear his viewpoint—how he sees the problem. Respect his experience, ideas, and abilities even if you don't agree with them.

- Without blame or accusation, share with her your perception and how you see the problem.

- Discuss what happened. *Explain*: When you said/did _____ I felt/thought _____ . *Seek to understand by asking*: What did you mean by this? Be careful to remain focused on the problem, not the person. Empathize with her feelings, but remember to ask for facts.

- Get the facts straight and identify the problem. What's the issue that's causing the conflict? Restate back to the person what you understand him to be saying. Make sure both of you agree on this—and don't be surprised if actually there isn't any issue to resolve. Strangely, conflicts often boil down to personality clashes or personal preferences.

- Ask if she is accusing you of wrongdoing—of sin. If you have sinned, humble yourself by asking for forgiveness. If you haven't sinned, resist feeling guilty. Be encouraged by Paul's words, "Each one of us shall give account of himself to God. Therefore let us not judge one another anymore" (Rom. 14:12-13 New American Standard Bible).

- Work together to find a solution. Ask the person to suggest a way to resolve the conflict. Could each of you do one thing differently? Get behind the other person, knowing he is imperfect, just as you are. Show your acceptance by asking how you can support him.

- Be bold—pray together, asking God to give you love and understanding.

In the case of Abraham and Lot, a real problem needed a practical solution. They couldn't all remain crowded in the same location. They needed to part company. Sometimes this is necessary for the sake of all involved.

Contrary to what often happens, however, going our separate ways doesn't have to wound and scar those involved. Arguing, attacking, hurting, and gossiping should never accompany the decision to part, because we always have a choice. Will we let the bitterness and anger of our fallen nature dominate our response? Or can we handle differences in the Spirit, becoming more like Jesus as a result?

Daily Choices for the Growing Heart
Consider Conflict as an Opportunity to Grow

Your natural response to being misunderstood at work or by a family member can change when you learn to think of conflict as an opportunity to grow. However, don't deny how you feel, because that won't help. Take the next step, instead.

- Make the choice to grow. When someone has hurt your feelings or treated you badly, choose to respond by asking the Lord, "How can I grow through this? Do you want me to be more patient? More loving? More understanding? Even though I'm feeling hurt, what do you want to produce in me so I'll be more pleasing to you?"

- Determine to honor God. Ask the Lord, "How can I glorify you in this? By seeking to understand the other person? By extending grace and forgiveness to her? By denying Satan the triumph of producing bitterness and a simmering grudge in me?"

- Allow God to use you for good. Ask Him, "How can I be a blessing to this person? Is there something I don't know that's behind his attitude and behavior toward me? Is it really not my problem, but his? What can I do to help him know your love?"

Start thinking and praying like this, and you'll become more like the Lord. He didn't retaliate when people hurled insults at Him, He made no threats when He suffered at their hands, and He forgave their cruelty. No wonder God wants us to recognize the opportunity for growth whenever we encounter prickly people and sticky situations.

Seven

Seek to Know the Living God

As the deer pants for the water brooks, so pants my soul for You, O God. (Ps. 42:1 New King James Version)

My frustration grew as I sat trapped in bumper-to-bumper traffic, the late afternoon sun glaring through the windshield. I had only thirty minutes to drive across Portland to my doctor's appointment—and the time was going fast.

Trying to find something to be thankful for, I muttered, "Thank you, God, for an air-conditioned car." But my gratitude quickly turned to grumbling as I thought, *Why, oh why, didn't I bring my cell phone? Then I could at least call to explain that three accidents are clogging up the freeway and I'm going to be horribly late. What am I going to do?*

After stewing in frustration for ten minutes, a rather unorthodox solution popped into my head. *If I could just catch the attention of a driver inching along beside me, maybe I could ask him to call and explain why I'm late.*

Staring out the window I checked each car to see if the passenger window was open, the driver was looking my way, and that all-important cell phone was visible. I perched on my seat ready to wave, smile, or act like a monkey if that's what it took to catch somebody's attention, but it was hopeless. Dozens of cars slowly moved past, but not one person glanced in my direction.

Scribbling a message and the number to call on the back of an envelope, I waited, desperate for an opportunity to put my plan into action. *After all,* I reasoned, *if shipwreck survivors can shove a note into a bottle and toss it in the ocean hoping someone will rescue them, why can't I pass an envelope through an open window?* My idea went nowhere, however, because every window stayed tightly shut against the heat—except for one.

A small delivery truck drew alongside—its window open. Not only that, a teenager in the passenger seat idly gazed my way. Without hesitating, I rolled down my window and yelled, "Do either of you have a cell phone? Would you make a call for me?" Looking startled, they grinned and replied, "Sure." After telling them what to say, I called out the phone number.

"Hey," said the young driver, keeping one eye on traffic, "you must be going to see Dr. Robertson. That's where my mom works. She's his receptionist."

"Wow!" I shouted back, stunned at the "coincidence." "That's amazing."

Is God alive? I know He is. Does He want us to experience His presence? Absolutely. Out of the dozens of cars that passed me, God had one specially picked out. Grateful as I was, I'm sure His primary purpose wasn't to solve my problem but to remind me of who He is: the all-knowing, all-powerful, and all-loving God. The only one who is fully aware of what I face, what I feel, and what I need.

God isn't an abstract concept, but a living person, who sees, cares, and acts—even in traffic jams.

Getting to Know God

In spite of experiences like this, do you sometimes wonder if we're deluding ourselves when we talk about knowing and being known by God? Is it really possible? How can finite creatures remotely comprehend someone so far beyond human comprehension? The truth is we can't—not unless God chooses to reveal himself—which He has in various ways.

"God spoke at many times and in various ways," declares the author of Hebrews. God communicated through dreams, visions, and words given to men and women. He also revealed His nature through His names. In fact, the Old Testament gleams with the glory of who God is and what He has said and done.

In addition, the Bible tells us about Jesus, Immanuel—God with us. John writes, "In the beginning was the Word, and the Word was with God, and the Word was God.... The Word became flesh and made his dwelling among us" (John 1:1, 14). When the right time came, God chose to speak through His Son who is "the radiance of God's glory and the exact representation of his being" (Heb. 1:1-3).

When people speak truthfully and with the desire to be known, what they say reveals who they are. Their beliefs, character, and feelings are displayed. It's no different with God. He wanted us to know what He's like—so He chose a unique way to accomplish His purpose. He sent Jesus, the second person of the Trinity, to live on earth and show us the Father.

By looking at Jesus' actions and listening to His words, we see God in the flesh. Jesus affirmed this truth when He said to Thomas, "If you really knew me, you would know my Father as well." To Philip's request that He show them the Father, Jesus replied, "Anyone who has seen me has seen the Father" (John 14:6-9).

Jesus' compassion for the lost and hurting, His power to change lives, and His willingness to forgive and restore, tell us about a God who knows what our lives are like. This is no remote being, detached from our human heartaches. We are known, and invited to know this God whose love covers and cleanses and "makes the foulest clean." No wonder the words "Amazing grace, how sweet the sound ..." fill us with a profound sense of gratitude and a hunger to know Him more fully.

In School with Abraham

When Abraham started walking with God, he began as a spiritual baby, just like most of us. Once he responded to the divine call, however, he became an eager lifelong student in God's school for spiritual growth. Supervising the development of his prize student, God gradually revealed more and more of himself through what He said and did. In this way, Abraham's faith expanded and deepened step by step.

Because of Christ, our knowledge today of God's character and purposes is much greater than Abraham's limited understanding. By faith he looked far ahead, fully believing God would keep His promises. With God's complete revelation in our hands, we look back at the fulfillment of those promises. By responding to each fresh revelation with trust and obedience, Abraham grew to know and love God more fully. Our progress follows the same path.

God revealed vital truths about himself to Abraham many times—truths that can make a difference in our lives also. Let's look at two of these occasions. Using events in Abraham's life, God taught him that He is the great and faithful one from whom nothing is hidden and the Sovereign Lord who protects and rewards His own (Gen. 13:14-18; 15:1).

God Sees Everything

As a child, did you ever feel that your brother or sister pulled the wool over your mother's eyes? Were you ever unfairly blamed for ripping open a bag of potato chips or sneaking off with cookies that were cooling on the counter? My mother used to wish out loud that she had the wisdom of Solomon whenever she caught my older sister and me doing something we shouldn't. Not being God-fearing little angels, our strategy was to raise our voices, blame the other, lie through our teeth, and confuse poor Mum till she gave up trying to figure out who was to blame.

God never has to face what mothers regularly deal with. Why? Because He has the divine ability to see everything that happens—even if it's hidden in the dark, or in our minds. "Nothing in all creation is hidden from God's sight. Everything is uncovered and laid bare before the eyes of him to whom we must give account," declares Hebrews 4:13. In a moment of Spirit-given revelation, David wrote, "O Lord, you have searched me and you know me. You know when I sit and when I rise; you perceive my thoughts from afar. You discern my going out and my lying down; you are familiar with all my ways. Before a word is on my tongue you know it completely, O Lord" (Ps. 139:1-4).

Doesn't the fact that absolutely nothing is hidden from God, that He even knows what you're thinking, take your breath away? The sheer magnificence of God should boggle our minds—and as our knowledge of Him keeps growing, it will.

The fact that nothing is hidden from God is amply borne out in the story of Abraham. After he decided they should part, Abraham invited Lot to choose where he wanted to go. Lot looked up, realized he had the opportunity of a lifetime, and without hesitation chose the best land for himself. Packing up his possessions and his household, he left for those greener pastures—or so he thought.

It seems the dust had barely disappeared off the horizon before God spoke. He hadn't missed anything: He saw Abraham's trusting attitude, his gracious handling of a potentially ugly situation, and the ungrateful, selfish behavior of Lot.

Revealing His knowledge of all that had transpired, maybe God said, "Okay, Abraham. You're not going to lose out to that little whippersnapper. Now you lift up *your* eyes from where you are and look north and south, east and west. *All* the land that you see I will give to you and your offspring forever. I, the God who sees your heart, your attitude, and your willing sacrifice, the One whose promises never fail, has spoken" (Gen. 13:14-17, my paraphrase).

One of the names of God is *El Roi*, "the God who sees me." The first time in Scripture God was called El Roi was when the Lord spoke to Hagar, Sarah's Egyptian servant, after she ran away. Seeing Hagar frightened, lonely, perhaps even defiant, God nevertheless assured her that both she and her unborn son had a future greater than she could imagine. Her life was not at an end, the God who sees everything would protect her (Gen. 16:7-16).

Job said of God, "He knows the way that I take" (23:10). This is always the case. God saw Abraham's encounter with Lot, Hagar's despair in the desert, and He sees our struggles today. Writing in *Christian Theology*, Millard Erickson says, "God is not a bureau or a department, a machine or a computer that automatically supplies the needs of people. He is a knowing, loving, good Father. He can be approached. He can be spoken to, and He in turn speaks."[1]

Think about the God who sees, the one who is omniscient and omnipresent—all-knowing and present everywhere. He misses nothing that is happening in your life—nor is He indifferent to your fear, confusion, anger, or struggles with loss. Let your heart and mind be awed and stirred by the fact that you belong to a personal, loving God who sees, cares, and who will act to meet your need as you bring it before Him.

- As you think about a situation you're dealing with, what genuine comfort or joy does this truth about God give you? Try to express your heart's response to God.

God Protects and Rewards

What are *you* afraid of? One friend, approaching forty, fears her chances of getting married and becoming a mother are slipping away. Another fears her long-term marriage might end soon. Several women I care about are battling cancer, concerned about what lies ahead for them and their families. Another wonders about her future ministry—has God put her on the shelf? Will she finish well, or soon fizzle out?

Taking our eyes off God and fixing them on our circumstances brings us face to face with frightening emotions. Abraham was no different.

Some time after Lot had settled in Sodom, war engulfed the land. Lot and his family, along with everyone else living in Sodom, were captured and marched off as slaves. Hearing about the fate of his relatives, Abraham gave chase against overwhelming odds, rescuing all the captives.

Returning from the battle, two people met him: the godly Melchizedek, "the priest of God Most High," and the ungodly king of Sodom. Melchizedek blessed Abraham. In turn, Abraham gave him a tenth of all the goods he'd recovered.

The king of Sodom insisted that Abraham should keep everything he'd recovered—except for the people—but Abraham refused. He'd learned his lesson in Egypt. If God wanted to prosper him, He could, but he wouldn't take so much as a thread or a shoelace, or anything else, so that the king of Sodom could never say, "I have made Abram rich" (Gen. 14:23).

After this event, God spoke in a vision to Abraham (Gen. 15:1). Why then? What had He seen that prompted Him to come with words of assurance? What did He want to reveal to Abraham about himself—and what can we learn from His revelation?

Abraham's Struggles

Wouldn't it be comforting if our struggles came one at a time, spaced far between, so we could recover from one before another hit? Unfortunately, this doesn't always happen. Often they come fast and furious, one on top of the other, as Abraham experienced.

His courageous rescue of Lot had put him and his family in danger of being attacked. If the warring kings returned, he would no doubt be at the top of their hit list. Refusing to cash in on his chance to profit from the battle was another issue Abraham probably struggled with. He'd shown his reliance on God to provide for him— but nevertheless, he'd lost out financially. In addition, his heartache over not having a son weighed on him—especially since God had promised this would happen.

When everything goes well, life seems good and we're grateful to God for blessing us. Get buried under a pile of problems, however, and our human tendency is to become like Abraham: despondent and fearful. Yet God allows these times for a reason. When He seems distant and our circumstances seem dark, He's preparing us to know Him in a new way.

This is what happened with Abraham. His need made him spiritually ready to receive what God wanted to teach him. Stepping in to give comfort, hope, and courage, God enlarged Abraham's vision of Himself. He also commanded, "Do not be afraid." Why not? On what grounds? Because He, the Sovereign Lord, was Abraham's shield and protection from evil.

God addressed Abraham's immediate need for a sense of security, but He also taught an unchanging spiritual principle: He is God Most High, the sovereign ruler of the universe. Because of who He is, He is able not only to protect from evil but also to "do superabundantly, far over *and* above all that we [dare] ask or think—infinitely beyond our highest prayers, desires, thoughts, hopes or dreams" (Eph. 3:20b AMP). He is our shield, and our reward—our source of peace, joy, and purpose.

- Are you struggling with some fear today? Do you have an enemy? Are you facing financial problems? Is your heart aching over a family issue? What comfort do you find in knowing that God himself is your shield and great reward?

Hungering for God

Can you remember when you first came to Christ? Did you know much about Him? Do you know more now? As a new believer, I understood only the most basic facts: God existed, He loved me, and Jesus died to save me from the penalty of sin. By confessing my sin and accepting His death on my behalf, I was reborn spiritually and entered God's family.

In those early days when I was a baby Christian, God put two longings within me: to know more *about* Him, and to *know Him* as much as I could. Digging into the Bible and learning *about* God thrilled me. Whether I studied on my own, in small groups, or listened to someone teaching, there was always something new to learn—or as was often the case, to relearn and put into practice.

It blew my mind to think that this God—who has always existed, created everything, knows everything, and can do whatever He pleases—actually loved me enough to break into my puny little life. I've never stopped marveling at this fact. Studying His Word fed my mind and gave me the knowledge I needed for a solid faith, but I wanted more than facts—I wanted a heart on fire for God.

Reading books about spiritual giants of earlier years such as Hudson Taylor, Jim Elliot, George Muller, Amy Carmichael, and A. W. Tozer inspired me. Their longing for God increased my desire to know Him. Their experience of His reality left me completely convinced that He is alive and active today.

Driving to work, I'd sing to God, sometimes so passionately tears rolled down my cheeks. Whatever hymns came to mind: "Worthy, O Lamb of God art Thou, that every knee to Thee should bow"; "When I survey the wondrous Cross on which the Prince of Glory died, my richest gain I count but loss and pour contempt on all my pride"; "Jesus, Thou joy of loving hearts, Thou fount of life, Thou light of men. From the best bliss that earth imparts, we turn unfilled to Thee again"—they filled me with so much love for God I thought my heart would burst.

Earnestly I Seek You ...

Augustine, one of the church fathers, said, "Thou hast formed us for Thyself, and our hearts are restless till they find rest in Thee." As Christ's followers, we've been created for His glory, to bring Him delight, to worship and rejoice in Him. This is our privilege and a hidden, bottomless source of satisfaction. David exclaimed, "O God, you are my God, earnestly I seek you; my soul thirsts for you, my body longs for you, in a dry and weary land where there is no water" (Ps. 63:1).

Can you sense David's heart desire? His earnest longing and awareness that only God could satisfy his spiritual thirst? Can you identify with his passion? I can. Unfortunately, however, I can also identify with feeling that all too often I'm wandering in a dry and weary land.

The spiritual thrills I experienced in the early days of my walk with God happened a long time ago. Has every day since been the same? I wish I could say, "Yes, my heart constantly pulsates with the passion for God that gripped me back then." Often it does—and I fall to my knees or burst out singing songs of adoration. Too frequently, however, thoughts of God simmer on the back burner of my mind. I know He's there, but instead of drawing close, I tolerate the sense of distance I feel. Why? Not because He's changed or has become less worthy of being loved with everything that is in me—but because I've allowed my glowing heart to grow cool.

Is this what I want? No. A hundred times NO. I truly long to say with David, "My heart is steadfast, O God; I will sing and make music with all my soul" (Ps. 108:1). I do want my life to throb with the same passion Paul expressed: "I count everything as loss compared to the possession of the priceless privilege—the overwhelming preciousness, the surpassing worth and supreme advantage—of knowing Christ Jesus my Lord, *and* of progressively becoming more deeply *and* intimately acquainted with Him, of perceiving *and* recognizing *and* understanding Him more fully *and* clearly" (Phil. 3:8 AMP).

So you may well ask, what's my problem?

Why do I grow distant and spiritually apathetic? And what causes other Christians, perhaps you too, also to struggle with spiritual apathy? The reasons vary, but four areas are often found at the root of our problem: lack of discipline, lack of comprehending God's greatness, lack of putting God first, and lack of moral purity.

God doesn't leave us to overcome our own weaknesses, however. He provides practical hands-on remedies throughout His Word. Let's look at some of these, knowing that "the eyes of the Lord range throughout the earth to strengthen those whose hearts are fully committed to him" (2 Chron. 16:9).

How Do I Increase My Hunger for God?

1. Check Out Your Self-Discipline

Despite my heartfelt desires, some days the newspaper catches my eye before I grab my Bible. Other times, I quickly check my e-mail, only to get engrossed in writing to a friend or reading breaking news. I might read a few devotionals, spend time in the Word, even journal my thoughts, but then suddenly remember I need to make a phone call. What happens to time for worship and prayer, to deepening intimacy with God, to hearing Him speak to my heart about a burden I'm carrying? It vanishes.

Without a doubt, if you're a naturally disciplined person, you'll find spending time with God easier to accomplish than someone who can hardly remember where she last saw her Bible and journal. Don't assume, however, that reading the Bible and praying every day guarantees a passionate love for God. It might—and this is certainly what God desires. Then again, this good habit might simply become a mindless routine you follow every day, much like brushing your teeth or washing your face.

God's Remedy:

While "religious" activities in and of themselves don't necessarily produce spiritual fervor, they do give the Holy Spirit an opportunity to speak. Psalm 1 poetically describes what occurs in us if we delight in the law of the Lord and meditate on it day and night. Little by little, we become "like a tree planted by streams of water, which yields its fruit in season and whose leaf does not wither."

Do you yearn for strong, spiritually stable roots? Do you long to produce spiritual fruit, the evidence of God's life within you? Are you tired of withering instead of flourishing? Then it's time to combat the creeping stranglehold of spiritual apathy and put Psalm 1 into action. To do this, commit yourself to specifics:

- *Take time to read the law of the Lord.* When will you do this? Where? For how long?

- *Pray over it.* When will you do this? Where? For how long?

- *Meditate on it day and night.* How will you do this? When? For how long?

Ask a friend to hold you accountable—to call once a week and ask the hard questions: "Are you being obedient and following through? What's happening as you earnestly seek God?" Pray for God to give you a hunger for himself. If you're serious, He will.

Lord, I'm not the regimented sort, but would you give me the desire to be self-controlled and self-disciplined? Remind me every time I'm tempted to say yes to whatever pops into my mind, that I'm saying no to what I most desire—staying passionately close to you. Help me to be humble enough to ask a friend to hold me accountable.

2. Increase Your Knowledge of God's Greatness

When the Pharisees asked Jesus what was the greatest commandment, He replied, "Love the Lord your God with all your heart and with all your soul and with all your *mind*" (Matt. 22:35-37). Exhilarating as it is to enjoy warm fuzzy feelings whenever we think of the Lord, feelings alone won't hold us steady when life turns rough. Aim to increase your knowledge of God. What is He like? What has He promised to do for us? This is essential information.

In writing to the Corinthians, Paul emphasized the importance of knowing *what* we believe when he said, "Do you not *know* ..."; "I do not want you to be *ignorant* of ..."; "I want to *remind* you ..." (1 Cor. 9:24; 10:1; 15:1). Peter also urged Christians to "grow in the grace and *knowledge* of our Lord and Savior Jesus Christ" (2 Pet. 3:18). The early Christians needed to *know* what they believed so they could pass it on. We have the same responsibility.

God's Remedy:

A deeper desire *for* God is fed by a growing knowledge *of* Him. The more we respond to what He teaches us about himself and the more we understand His ways, the more we desire *Him*. Reading, thinking about, and delighting in His character is like adding a fast-burning log to a dying fire—it ignites our passion.

My heart is stirred to the depths by the words, "The Lord, the Lord, the compassionate and gracious God, slow to anger, abounding in love and faithfulness, maintaining love to thousands, and forgiving wickedness, rebellion and sin" (Exod. 34:6-7). Pause here for a moment. Let yourself be filled with wonder at these statements. Do we truly marvel at this? Never before in history—until Jesus came—was such a wonder revealed.

God is compassionate—He feels with us. He is gracious—His undeserved favor flows toward us. Slow to anger—not quick to zap His stubborn little sheep into submission, He abounds in such love that no nook or cranny of our lives remains untouched. He forgives—willingly paying an awful price on the cross to wipe away all evidence of our wickedness, rebellion, and sin. What a God we have.

To build and maintain a passionate love for God, we have to increase both our knowledge and awareness of Him. Here are some ways to do this:

- Deliberately focus your mind on a characteristic of God—perhaps a favorite one, or one you haven't thought much about. You might choose to concentrate on His mercy, wisdom, or majesty. Do this as you drive to work, take care of ordinary chores, or as you prepare to go to church. You don't have to go away from other people to do this—let your mind be a secret inner sanctuary where you draw close to God in privacy.

- As you jog around your neighborhood or drive down a tree-lined street, pull your mind away from all you have to do. Instead, marvel at God's creation. Think about His power as Creator, His sovereign rule over all He's made, His goodness evidenced by the beauty and color that surrounds you.

- Set aside some time on Sundays for God alone—in addition to attending church. God ordained that one day of each week be different from the rest. If you don't have to work on Sunday, curl up with your Bible for a quiet half-hour or longer retreat with the Lord. If you do work on Sundays, carve out time another day. Most of us have no trouble feeding our physical appetites—we buy and fix food, sleep late, watch TV, or go to a ball game. What do we do to sharpen our spiritual appetites?

Lord, give me a fresh appetite for yourself. Help me grow to know you, think about you, and be open to a sense of wonder. Make the psalmist's words true of me: "I meditate on your precepts and consider your ways. I delight in your decrees; I will not neglect your word" (Ps. 119:15-16).

3. Determine to Put God in First Place

In his book *The Pursuit of God*, pastor and author A. W. Tozer asked the question, "Why do some people seem to have an especially close relationship with God?"[2] That question often echoes in my mind.

Talking to Glenda, a young and successful career woman, I inquired about her walk with the Lord. "I've been drifting for several years," she admitted. "Instead of putting my relationship with God first, I just ignored Him and had fun running around with friends. I haven't attended church or prayed for ages. Recently, though, I've begun to wonder where my life is going."

Glenda had come to faith in Christ as a child, she said. She'd walked with Him through all the challenges of high school and college—but then slowly let her desire for God slip away as she climbed the career ladder. Then one day she recognized something stirring in her. She felt lonely for God and longed to return to the closeness with Him that had once marked her life.

Answering his question, "Why do some people have an especially close relationship with God?" Tozer suggests that those who walk close to God have one vital quality in common: *spiritual receptivity*. Referring to Christians of a previous day, he comments, "Something in them ... urged them Godward. They had spiritual awareness and they went on to cultivate it until it became the biggest thing in their lives. They differed from the average person in that when they felt the inward longing, *they did something about it*."

God's Remedy:

Describing how she responded to her renewed desire for fellowship with God, Glenda said, "I decided to talk to John, a local pastor, who has been a powerful influence in my life. I also began reading the Psalms, and started back to church. Later I sought out a spiritual mentor who is helping me move forward with the Lord."

How the Spirit works in us is a mystery—that He does is a thrilling fact. Glenda is experiencing this. Responding to the Spirit's gentle voice, she's steadily returning to a God-centered life.

No matter how long we drift or how spiritually lukewarm we become, God continues to call us back to a fresh and growing love relationship with Him. That He began a good work in us proves He will faithfully complete it (Phil. 1:6). To experience this, however, we must respond to God and take action. To honor God's rightful authority over your will and wishes, consider the following:

- Analyze where God is on your list of priorities. Are there other activities, desires, or relationships that matter more to you than pleasing God? Be willing to acknowledge the truth—God won't be surprised. Ask Him to break their attraction and replace it with a hunger to please Him.

- Think about those priorities that rank higher than pleasing God. How might He want you to reorder these? Pray for insight, then write out what you feel are God's values for you at this time in your life.

- Reordering your life to put God in first place doesn't happen without making some deliberate decisions. Which ones do you need to make?

Renewing a fresh and growing walk with God takes effort, patience, and obedience. If you've grown cold, pour out your heart to God. Pray for the Holy Spirit to rekindle your love, and commit yourself to taking whatever steps He points out to you.

Lord, too often my desire for you is drowned out by other attractions. I want to enjoy a spiritually intimate relationship with you, but I struggle to relinquish other idols. Inflame my heart so nothing and no one matters more to me than you. Help me turn from idols to you, the living God.

4. Value Moral Purity

Think about this real-life situation:

"Some of us from work are going to celebrate the completion of a project by going away for the weekend. Everyone will be bringing a guest. How would it be wrong for me to ask a male friend to go with me? There's nothing sexual going on between us, so what's the problem with sharing a room? I feel so childish not allowing my friend to spend the night in my room."

Or this one:

"A friend and I liked the looks of two guys we saw at a concert. They must have seen us looking at them because they came over and we had a drink with them. We knew one of them was married, but both of us wanted to kiss him because he was the cutest. My friend did—and boy, did I feel jealous. What's wrong with that? It was only a kiss—nothing more."

Contrast those two situations with this:

When Isaiah saw God's glory, he cried out with horror at his own sin, "My doom is sealed, for I am a foul-mouthed sinner" (Isa. 6:5 TLB). Peter responded to Jesus in the same way: "Go away from me, Lord; I am a sinful man!" (Luke 5:8). Paul, in a moment of soul-searching honesty, described himself as the greatest of sinners.

Spiritual indifference inevitably occurs when we lower the standard God calls us to live by. Grieving the Holy Spirit who lives in us, we can easily excuse our attitudes and behavior, blending in seamlessly with those who have no desire for God. Living like this we lose our sensitivity to God's holiness and hatred of sin, our hunger to know Him leaves, and a spiritual coldness settles on our hearts like a chilling fog.

God's Remedy:

Can we really avoid going along with today's culture? Is it possible to hold ourselves to God's standard in a society that shamelessly says whatever you want to do, go ahead and do it? Hard as it is to stand against the pull of our world, our old nature, and our relentless Enemy, we have to say, "Yes, with God's help, *and my cooperation*, it is possible to live—and enjoy—a sexually moral life."

What's the key?

- Pray for a passionate determination to honor God that far outweighs your desire to be accepted and a part of the crowd. "Put to death, therefore, whatever belongs to your earthly nature: sexual immorality, impurity, lust, evil desires and greed.... You *used to* walk in these ways, in the life you once lived. *But now* you must rid yourselves of all such things" (Col. 3:5-8). If necessary, look for new friends who share your desire to honor God.

- Talk over the moral dilemmas you encounter with a mature Christian. Ask your friend to speak frankly, showing you what Scripture teaches.

- Commit yourself to following what God says—even if it cuts against what you think you want to do. Hold to His plumb line of moral purity, not what others say or do.

Lord, forgive my indifference to sin. Help me grieve when I turn away from Your plumb line of moral purity. Deepen my gratitude for salvation and all it means, both now and for eternity. Sear into my heart the amazing fact that through Jesus Christ, I have been made holy once and for all.

- Do you identify with any of these reasons for spiritual apathy? Can you think of others? Why not take a few minutes to reflect on your hunger for God. How would you describe your desire for Him right now? I know this isn't a comfortable question—but answer it as best as you can.

- What do you think has contributed to where you are?

- Has the Spirit shown you some action, attitude, or desire that is robbing you of hunger for God? What is it, and what will you do about it?

Finding Hope

Are you—am I—miserable failures if, in all honesty, we have to confess that our passion for God ebbs and flows? Our Enemy would certainly try to make us believe this. Yet God never views us as hopeless. He knows us better than we know ourselves and understands "how we are formed, he remembers that we are dust." Far from condemning our fluctuating commitment, He is a loving Father who "has compassion on his children ... on those who fear him" (Ps. 103:13-14).

David talks about God's Word "*reviving* the soul" (Ps. 19:7). He also acknowledges that our souls need "*restoring*" (Ps. 23:2-3). Another writer of psalms cries out in a burst of honest self-appraisal, "Oh, that my ways were steadfast in obeying your decrees! Then I would not be put to shame when I consider all your commands" (Ps. 119:5-6).

Who would need reviving and restoring if we never ran out of spiritual vitality? The problem of the human heart turning away from the spring of living water is nothing new. God knows we need frequent reviving—much like the wilted flowers on my patio. Once overflowing their pots, my formerly vibrant geraniums, petunias, and dahlias now struggle to survive constant neglect. It's not that I don't think about watering them, I do—but it's only when I act on my thoughts that the poor plants revive.

We can think all we want to about our need to draw close to God, but we'll only be spiritually refreshed, renewed, and revived when we take action. Unlike potted plants, we choose whether or not to pour the living water of God's Word onto our parched souls.

"The Lord is my Shepherd, I shall not be in want," said David with gratitude and great joy. "He leads me beside quiet waters, He *restores* my soul." Jesus, the Good Shepherd, does the same for us.

When we wander away, He gently draws us back into fellowship with Him. When our souls are sick, He is there to restore our spiritual health. When life drains us spiritually dry, He replenishes our inner life with the joy of His presence. The Holy Spirit's power, fresh supplies of passion for God, and a new vision for what our lives can be, can come quickly. We only need to ask Him to restore our souls.

The "normal Christian life is a repeated process of restoration and renewal. Our joy is not static. It fluctuates with real life. It is vulnerable to Satan's attacks," writes John Piper in *Desiring God*.[3]

Would anyone disagree?

What a relief to know that our acceptance with God is not based on our perfection or ability to love Him perfectly, but on His sacrificial love for us. Let's rejoice with Jude, who wrote, "To those who have been called, who are loved by God the Father and kept by Jesus Christ.... To him who is able to keep you from falling and to present you before his glorious presence without fault and with great joy—to the only God our Savior be glory, majesty, power and authority, through Jesus Christ our Lord, before all ages, now and forevermore! Amen" (Jude 1:24-25).

Daily Choices for the Growing Heart
Seek to Know the Living God

Your hunger for God is a gift from Him. Like all gifts, however, it must be received and used in order to bless the recipient. Our desire for God comes from the working of the Holy Spirit within us, but we must respond to His stirrings. Reflect on the following attitudes that throbbed in the hearts of the psalmists—then prayerfully ask God for these same qualities to flood your soul.

- Desire for Him: "Give me an undivided heart that I may fear your name" (Ps. 86:11).
- Devotion to Him: "I seek you with all my heart; do not let me stray" (Ps. 119:10).
- Discipline, motivated by love for Him: "I will be careful to lead a blameless life.... I will set before my eyes no vile thing" (Ps. 101:2-3).
- Delight in Him: "I run in the path of your commands, for you have set my heart free" (Ps. 119:32).

Eight

Depend on God's Strength, Not Your Own

We are a new creation in Christ, and we need to daily appropriate that truth by faith.[1]

"God is showing me a few things about myself when I take Laura to swimming lessons," said Jenny, laughing. "Laura is three years old and determined to do everything by herself. When she gets in the pool, she dog-paddles with all her might but can't stay afloat for very long. When I reach out to help her, though, she'll have none of it. She shouts, 'Self, self!' She'll only call out, 'Mommy, help; Mommy, help!' when she's about to sink.

"I guess I'm the same way with God," Jenny added with a rueful grin.

Whether we're three, twenty-three, or sixty-three, our human tendency is to behave just like Laura. When we find ourselves plunged into life's deep waters, what happens? Don't we instinctively depend on ourselves, using our personality, powers of persuasion, abilities, or quick thinking to handle whatever comes?

Only when the inevitable happens—our emotional strength runs out, we recognize we don't have the power to change a situation, or another person's behavior pushes us to the brink of despair—do we finally come to our senses, remembering God wants us to handle life in His strength, not our own.

Sadly, sometimes we won't come to our senses and cry out to God for help. Determined to figure out what to do by ourselves, we ignore God's power to help us find the best solution. We depend on our own wisdom, decide what we want to do, and dismiss or downplay the likely consequences. Helen chose this path when she realized she was bored with her husband and her marriage.

"I know God hates divorce," she said, "but I'm ready to leave Dave and live my own life. Dave's a nice person, but he's so dull." Despite the concern of more spiritually mature friends in her church, Helen was determined to do what she wanted. "God will forgive me, and I can't help what other people think. Dave will get over it and probably marry again. I'm going to do what I want with my life."

Helen's refusal to get counseling and work on her marriage, her casual dismissal of God, and her callous indifference to the way she would devastate Dave's life runs totally counter to how we're called to live. Yet every one of us might act like her, should we choose to live under the control of our old sinful nature rather than in obedience to God's Spirit.

When we're determined to depend on our own wisdom and go our own way, we grieve God's heart. We sow hurtful seeds that can never be totally uprooted. Even though God mercifully forgives when we repent, consequences often hover like shadows, haunting the rest of our lives. Because of the lifelong, and perhaps eternal, impact of our choices, it's vital that we learn what it means to live under the Spirit's guidance, depending on God's strength.

To grow in spiritual maturity, we must know some spiritual basics: What's the difference between the old and new nature? Who were we before we belonged to Christ? Who are we now? How should this affect the way we see ourselves, or the way we handle our emotions, or process our thoughts and make decisions? The door to spiritually effective and joy-filled living opens when we understand these questions and their answers.

God, who has called us to live under the Spirit's control, has also provided all the resources we need to make this possible (2 Pet. 1:3). A clear grasp of these truths frees us from the depressing cycle of trying our best to measure up to a standard of impossible perfection, then failing and feeling guilty—followed by trying harder or giving up the struggle altogether. This isn't God's plan for you or me, or for anybody.

God's desire is that we enjoy a love-based, not a guilt-based, relationship with Him. Once we have this, we can walk through life delighting in the fact that nothing, not even our human weaknesses, can separate us from His embrace.

Asking the Holy Spirit to open our understanding, let's explore these important principles using Sarah, Abraham, and Hagar as our examples. We'll see what happens when our sinful nature is in control, in contrast with walking in obedience to the Spirit.

- My way, God's way—what difference does it make?
- Who am I?
- How do I live under the Spirit's control?

My Way, God's Way—What Difference Does It Make?

The next major development in Abraham's journey provides a vivid example of what happens when we attempt to handle life without God's help. Sarah manipulated Abraham, demanding what she wanted in no uncertain terms. Surprised, Abraham capitulated. Hagar, watching this, then miscalculated the situation, trying some manipulation of her own.

I Want What I Want, NOW

Chapter 16 of Genesis opens with Sarah at the end of her rope. Gripped by the tension of waiting ten long years for the promised son, she was desperate. She'd had enough of waiting for God. Where was He? Why hadn't He kept His promise by now? Slowly sinking under the weight of her emotions, Sarah was frustrated, impatient, disappointed, and wrestling with major stress.

Despite God's initial promise that Abraham would have an heir, nothing had happened. God had even expanded on His promise several times, and still she and Abraham remained in exactly the same situation as ever—childless. Giving up hope that she would ever have a son in the normal way, Sarah determined to get what she wanted one way or another—and watch out, anyone who tried to stand in her way.

After chewing over the situation endlessly, a "brilliant" solution finally started to form in her mind. She'd pressure Abraham to have a child by Hagar, her slave—knowing that any son born to Abraham would be hers to keep. This was how barren women became mothers according to the culture of that time, so why not? After all, she might have reasoned as people mistakenly do today: *Doesn't God help those who help themselves?*

Perhaps Sarah's thinking went the way ours does all too often: *Since God hasn't answered my prayer so far, it's obvious He's never going to. I'm not going to have a child by sitting around twiddling my thumbs. So I have two choices: either give up what I long for or get my husband to see it my way.*

For her plan to succeed, Sarah had to get Abraham on board. How she did this, we're not told. As most females know, sometimes womanly wiles, tears, and seeming helplessness work wonders on the male sex. At other times, an assertive, demanding woman can cause a confused man to cower and capitulate. Either way, it's called manipulation.

Sarah felt secure in her position as Abraham's wife. She knew he loved her, and she loved him. She also was aware of the enormous influence and power a wife can have over her husband. Counting on that power rather than on God, she probably took a deep breath and plunged in, telling Abraham flat out: "The Lord has kept me from having children. Go sleep with my maidservant; perhaps I can build a family through her."

Her analysis of the situation was correct—in one way. God *had* kept her from becoming pregnant at that time. However, her assumption that she would never have a child was completely wrong. God would fulfill His promise and meet the desire of her heart. She would have a child—but according to His divine plan and timetable, not hers.

To be fair to Sarah, God had never named her as the mother of Abraham's promised heir. In fact, it would be another thirteen years before she would know this. God had reserved a unique blessing and privilege for her—yet she was convinced she'd never experience the fulfillment of her greatest desire. Lacking in strong faith, and basing her decision on faulty assumptions, Sarah depended on her own power to get what she wanted.

- Do you identify with Sarah? Have you waited years and years for a "slow-moving" God to meet the desire of your heart? Has this left you frustrated, resentful, or despairing, like Sarah? Take a few moments to reflect on these questions. Express your longing as a prayer, honestly telling God how you feel.

- Strong desires can tempt any of us to manipulate circumstances, pressure a family member or friend, or use our own power to get what we want. Is this happening in your life? Or are you responding to your waiting time with God-given wisdom? James describes this wisdom as "first of all pure; then peace-loving, considerate, submissive, full of mercy and good fruit, impartial and sincere" (James 3:17). What would you say?

Wrong as Sarah was to take things into her own hands, it's not difficult to see why she hatched such a desperate scheme. Combine her reasonable expectations based on God's promises, mix them with a big dose of womanly yearning, add constant disappointment, and what would you expect? She thought she knew what God would do and when He would do it—a mistake we all make. When He didn't perform to her expectations, she turned resentful and rebellious, determined to get what she wanted at any cost.

This meant pressuring Abraham to go along with her plan, not God's.

I Want Peace at Any Price

Sarah spelled out exactly what she wanted. Did Abraham protest? Did he encourage his wife's faith by urging, "Let's wait for God to act. We can trust Him to give us a son in His perfect timing. This isn't the way God wants us to meet the desires of our heart." No. He immediately agreed. He caved in. Without a word of dissent, he capitulated.

Nothing indicates Abraham stopped to consider whether Sarah's plan was right or wrong. He doesn't seem to have given a thought to the possible consequences, nor does he assert his responsibility as the spiritual leader of his household. Could he have thought, perhaps, *Well, why not? It's my right, although I can't believe my wife would suggest such a thing. If she doesn't mind, why should I protest? Maybe ...*

Whatever he thought, and even if he rationalized that this was perfectly acceptable in their culture, Abraham failed to act as he should. He didn't seek God's will. He didn't wait for God's direction. Nor did he affirm to Sarah his conviction that God was able to fulfill His promise no matter how much time went by.

Abraham's response shows that he chose to avoid conflict, protecting himself from a possible verbal assault launched by Sarah. Like many men, he'd probably learned over the years how to maintain peace with his wife.

Giving in to pressure and neglecting to seek God's perspective is likely to bring painful consequences for everyone involved. By abdicating our responsibility to stand up for what is right, we lose God's blessing. We also lose the ability to be a spiritual influence on others, and we damage our fellowship with God. This is the price Abraham paid: having no encounter with the Sovereign Lord for another thirteen years (Gen. 17).

David Prior, author of *Living by Faith,* suggests we measure any pressure we feel or advice we're given against this question: "Does this encourage me to move forward in faith, or does it appeal instead to my natural desires for the security of the familiar, the esteem of others, and the satisfaction of creature comforts?"[2]

- As you think of advice you're receiving, or the inward pressure you're feeling to take certain actions, how does this question help you decide what to do?

Both Sarah and Abraham failed to apply this spiritual measuring stick. Abraham carried out Sarah's scheme, giving her the son she wanted through Hagar. However, their troubles had just begun.

I Want to Be Someone

Delighted that her scheme had worked, Sarah must have thought, *This has to be from the Lord. How else could it have turned out like this?* That kind of thinking is dangerous. Just because our human scheming results in what we want doesn't mean God is in it—as Sarah soon found out.

Once Hagar knew she was pregnant, she, too, began to scheme. She was quick to see that her status and future had changed for the better. Wanting to wring every drop of advantage from this new situation, Hagar may have thought, *I'm no longer some insignificant slave; I'm having the master's child. My son will be his heir. That old woman Sarah is barren, and if I'm smart, who knows what might happen?*

Swollen with self-importance, Hagar began to look down on Sarah. Acting cocky and arrogant, this young immature girl strutted around boasting of her new position in the household. Furious at what was happening, Sarah exploded.

And whom did she blame for being despised by this uppity slave girl? None other than Abraham. Can't you imagine her boiling over with jealousy, anger, and frustration? "If you hadn't agreed to do what I told you to do, this would never have happened, Abraham. Why didn't you act like a man and stand up to me? This is all your fault. May God judge who is wrong and who is right."

In response, Abraham once again caved in. No doubt feeling unfairly accused and thoroughly irritated, he snaps, "Do what you want with her." He isn't going to take any responsibility for the situation. Feeling justified in punishing Hagar, Sarah makes her life a misery. Seeing her dreams of status and power dashed, Hagar runs away, unable to cope any longer. What a mess.

Paul warned the Galatians that when they followed the desires of their sinful nature, their lives would produce these evil results: sexual immorality, impure thoughts, eagerness for lustful pleasure, idolatry ... hostility, quarreling, jealousy, outbursts of anger, selfish ambition, divisions (Gal. 5:19-20 NLT). Leaving God out of the picture and depending on ourselves to meet our needs and solve our problems is a temptation we all face. When we choose to do this, we end up acting just like Sarah, Abraham, and Hagar. Think about their choices:

- Abraham practiced monogamy until Sarah talked him into having sex with Hagar. They both used, and abused, another human being for their own purposes. We, too, might use people, taking selfish advantage of others at work, of our own family or friends, even those at church, in order to gain what we want.

- Sarah made having a child her idol. She gave up trusting God and stopped at nothing to get what she wanted. We might do the same if we obsess over having a fancier house or car, a more prominent position, or pushing our kids to be better than anyone else's.

- Sarah was angry when her plans backfired. Instead of admitting guilt for her part in causing the problem, she blamed both Abraham and Hagar. We sin in the same way if we refuse to admit our fault in a quarrel or division, choosing to cast blame on others.

- Hagar's ambition outstripped her ability to assess her situation accurately. She wanted to be someone, but got tripped up by her pride and ego. We also can become inflated with who we think we are, despising those who don't meet our standards for looks, education, or accomplishments. In our striving for recognition, we lose sight of the fact that everything we are and have is a gift from God.

- As you reflect on this dismal story of what happens when God is ignored, is the Spirit bringing something to mind that you need to think and pray about? Be honest with yourself, jotting down whatever is bothering you. Then give yourself time to hear what God wants to say.

Who Am I?

None of us who long to walk with God has any real desire to be under the control of our old nature, but it happens, for various reasons. "Satan is opposed to our maturity and will do anything he can to keep us from realizing who we are and what we have in Christ," states Neil Anderson.[3]

Living under the Spirit's control and experiencing what God has promised is possible, but doesn't happen automatically. To grow to the maturity God intends, we need to understand what the Bible means when it describes the old and new natures. Then we need to go a step further, realizing who we *now* are in Christ and what this means in our daily lives. Let's review these biblical teachings by going back to the beginning.

The Old Has Gone, the New Has Come

When God created Adam, He made him alive both physically and spiritually. Furthermore, Adam was created in God's image, as we all are. This doesn't mean God has arms and legs like a human being. God is Spirit. Being made in His image means we have a mind, emotions, and will. We can think, we can feel, and we can choose—as God does.

In the beginning, God and Adam spent time together enjoying each other's company—nothing hindered their fellowship (Gen. 2). Adam didn't feel he had to hide from God, shrink from his failures, or wrestle with a guilt complex. He knew nothing about these struggles because he was perfect in every way.

In the joy of knowing God loved him, he lived daily with the profound awareness of being accepted, significant, and secure. Life was good, his heart at peace—until that fateful day when he followed Eve and disobeyed God. At that point everything changed, because Adam died spiritually—as God said he would (Gen. 2:16-17).

Did the terrible consequences of Adam's sin stop with him? Much as I wish they had, the answer is NO. Every person since Adam has been born spiritually dead, separated from God, *affected by* and *infected with* the sin virus. "When Adam sinned, sin entered the entire human race. Adam's sin brought death, so death spread to everyone, for everyone sinned" (Rom. 5:12 NLT).

Test this statement: Watch two-year-olds kick and scream when their will is thwarted; six-year-olds steal; sixteen-year-olds lie; adults sleep around with someone else's spouse, trash-talk about a co-worker, or claw their way to power and prestige. It becomes abundantly clear—not one of us has escaped the consequences of Adam's disobedience.

Each of us has a sinful nature, a bent toward living apart from God's direction. True, not everyone expresses this outwardly to the same degree—in fact, some people act so sweet and kind you wonder if they somehow escaped this universal infection. Yet in spite of what appears on the surface, at the core of our being, we all sing, "I'll do it my way," and that's how we live—unless we put our faith in Christ and choose to live under the Spirit's control.

Both Scripture and life experience tell us that from birth everyone has a sinful nature, but do you know what this is and how you can recognize the kind of behavior it prompts?

What Is the Sinful Nature?

The sinful nature is described in different terms depending on what version of the Bible you read. Terms such as "the old nature, human nature, the old self, the old man, the spirit of the world," or "the flesh," all refer to the same dismal spiritual condition common to everyone.

Thinking and reacting from an "I"-centered, or "self"-oriented focus are marks of the old nature. Decisions are based on what *I* want to do, what *I* want to have, what *I* think is best for *me*. *Self*-will, *self*-seeking, and *self*-conceit dominate the heart and determine the direction of our life. These are vividly illustrated in this latest episode of Abraham's journey.

In addition, the sinful nature, or "the flesh," is attracted to whatever is opposed to God, appealing to the physical senses and the need for significance and power over others. Paul says, "The sinful nature desires what is contrary to the Spirit.... They are in conflict with each other"; and "Those controlled by the sinful nature cannot please God" (Gal. 5:17; Rom. 8:8).

When the Bible refers to "the flesh," it doesn't mean the physical body—saying it is bad. True, it's through the body that our sin is frequently expressed, but in itself, the body is an incredible creation of God, who pronounced all He made "good."

Because of Adam's sin, however, the normal drives God built into us for our blessing and His glory have been corrupted. Now instead of valuing sexual intimacy as a beautiful expression of marital love, the sinful nature lusts for uncommitted sex. Instead of viewing work as a God-given gift and a way to provide for yourself and others, the sinful nature craves money and success to satisfy the longing for importance.

Understanding where the old nature comes from and how it's expressed is essential, but that's not the full picture. We also need to know that once we put our faith in Christ, we receive a new nature—one that is not corrupted by sin and marked by failure and guilt. Underlining this liberating truth, Paul joyously declares to every Christian: "You are *not* controlled by your sinful nature. You are controlled by the Spirit if you have the Spirit of God living in you" (Rom. 8:9 NLT).

Let's discover what that means.

What Is the New Nature?

When we are born spiritually by faith in Jesus Christ, God's Spirit comes to live in us and we receive a new nature. Because of the Cross, God declares that all things have become new in our relationship with Him. Instead of being spiritually dead, we are spiritually alive. We are a new creation in Christ, no longer condemned, or separated from God because of our sins (Eph. 2:1-5).

Speaking of what would happen when the Holy Spirit lived in people of faith, God promised, "I will give you a new heart and put a new spirit in you; I will remove from you your heart of stone and give you a heart of flesh. And I will put my Spirit in you and move you to follow my decrees" (Ezek. 36:26-27). Our new nature changes us from the inside out. We have new desires, make new decisions, and think new thoughts.

When my father came to Christ at the age of seventy, he looked back over his life, and commented, "Poppy, I realize that I thought more about what I wanted to do than how it affected your mother or you and your sisters." Without a new heart and a new mind, Dad would never have considered his going to the pub every night as self-centered and detrimental to our family life. With a renewed mind and perspective, he saw things he could never have grasped or admitted before.

The new nature is also energized to do what pleases God because His Spirit lives in us. "It is God who works in you to will and to act according to his good purpose" (Phil. 2:13). To act according to God's good purpose is to live under the Spirit's control, obedient to His will. This is the same as being "led by the Spirit" or "filled with the Spirit." Whatever terms we use, we're talking about our heart-longing to do and be only what pleases God, choosing to depend on His power, not our own.

Along with our new nature, at the time of our salvation, we receive a new standing in God's eyes. Seeing us wrapped in Christ's perfection, He accepts us unconditionally. No longer viewed as guilty sinners deserving eternal punishment, we are now His beloved children. When these truths hit home, how we look at ourselves and what happens in our lives inevitably changes.

Who Am I, Now That I'm in Christ?

Before he sinned, Adam felt totally accepted by God. He mattered—not because he was so wonderful but because God valued him. This gave Adam a profound sense of significance. He knew deep within himself that he was incredibly important to someone who cared, encouraged, and watched over his life.

This is God's message to your heart and mine.

He accepts you. You are secure in His never-ceasing love. You are significant to Him.

Now the barrier of sin has been removed; this is how God sees and feels toward you. In the same way that Adam enjoyed acceptance, security, and significance before he sinned, so can you and I. Why? Because we are in Christ, who makes us holy before God.

Scripture is full of statements that declare this amazing, life-changing truth. Here are just a few to nurture your heart and soul:

- *In Christ, I am accepted:*

  I am God's child (John 1:12).

  I have been justified—declared not guilty of sin (Rom. 5:1).

  I am a member of Christ's body (1 Cor. 12:27).

  I am a saint (Eph. 1:1).

I have access to God the Father through God the Spirit (Eph. 2:18).

- *In Christ, I am secure:*

    I am free forever from condemnation (Rom. 8:1).

    I am assured that God works for the good of those who love Him (Rom. 8:28).

    I will never be separated from the love of Christ (Rom. 8:35).

    I have been chosen, included in Christ, and sealed with the Spirit (Eph. 1:11-14).

    I can receive mercy and grace to help me in my time of need (Heb. 4:16).

    I am born of God and the Evil One cannot harm me (1 John 5:18).

- *In Christ, I am significant:*

    I am connected to Christ and a channel of His life to others (John 15:4).

    I have been chosen and appointed to bear fruit (John 15:16).

    I am God's temple; His Spirit lives in me (1 Cor. 3:16).

    I am God's fellow worker (2 Cor. 6:1).

    I am God's workmanship (Eph. 2:10).

    I can do all things through Christ who strengthens me (Phil. 4:13).[4]

If you're at all like me, you find it easy to read this list of statements without their meaning going any further than your brain.

If that's as far as we let these truths penetrate, however, we'll never experience their life-changing power.

God makes these declarations for a reason—they are meant to flood our hearts with joy, saturate our thoughts with Spirit-given confidence, and change how we respond and act in every circumstance.

- Take a few minutes to look back over these three lists. Choose one truth from each list and think about it. What difference would consciously believing this make in your life today? Write your response as a prayer note to God.

In Christ, I am accepted:
In Christ, I am secure:
In Christ, I am significant:

How Do I Live Under the Spirit's Control?

Have you ever asked yourself the question, "If I have a new nature, why do I struggle with the temptation to sin—and fail, all too often?" Don't despair. Scripture makes it abundantly clear that even after receiving the new nature, sin can still be a problem in our lives. John writes, "If we claim to be without sin, we deceive ourselves and the truth is not in us" (1 John 1:8). Paul also addressed our constant battle with sin saying, "Walk by the Spirit, and you will not carry out the desire of the flesh" (Gal. 5:16 NASB).

Clearly there is a conflict going on. Even though we're no longer under the control of our old sinful nature, sin still dwells in us. When we give in to the temptation to sin, bursting out in rage, stewing in self-pity, or massaging a grudge, we stunt our growth and *act like someone we're not.*

As believers, we no longer live in spiritual darkness. Sin shouldn't be able to yank us around as if we're helpless victims. We don't have to throw up our hands and say, "I can't help sinning!" We can. The person we once were doesn't exist. We're a new creation, children of God, people who have the Holy Spirit living in them—and because of this, God's power is available to us in every situation.

True, it often takes time to break free of old habitual responses. Yes, we do have to reprogram our minds by learning God's promises and counting on them. We do have to continually choose not to give in when our old nature whispers, "Oh, come on. You know you want to do this, so why not?" Growing more like Jesus takes effort and cooperation—but so does any victory.

Nations don't win wars by passively allowing the enemy to pound them to pieces. Wars are won by standing up and fighting with all the weapons at our disposal. This is no less true in the spiritual realm than in the physical.

Our enemies are frequently described as an evil threesome: the world, the flesh, and the devil.

- "The world" doesn't mean God's beautiful creation. In Scripture, "the world" represents the philosophies and values that people have apart from God—cravings for physical gratification outside of God's will; a restless greed that can never say, "I have enough"; an ego that boasts about itself and what it has and does (1 John 2:15-16).

- "The flesh" is that inner sinful nature that still wants to jerk us around. Using subtly enticing thoughts or powerful, overwhelming desires, the flesh battles to stay in control of our lives (Rom. 6:11-14).
- Satan, our third enemy, never gives up his onslaughts either. He attacks, sometimes through subtly distorting

God's character, as he did with Eve. Other times he acts as an "angel of light," hoping to deceive and lead astray. Frequently he comes as the great discourager, worming his way into our thinking and tempting us to doubt God's love and goodness (Gen. 3:1-7; 2 Cor. 11:14; Heb. 3:12-13).

With these three enemies seeking to devour and destroy our desire to please God, how could we possibly imagine we are able to overcome them by our own strength? Knowing there's no way we can, God has provided all the resources we need to fight and win.

Our resources begin with knowing God's Spirit lives in us, but that isn't sufficient unless we also know *how* to depend on God's strength when we're under attack. Here are three steps we have to take whenever we're spiritually attacked. To achieve victory:

1. Turn to God

Do this as soon as you realize you're depending on yourself, assessing what's happening from a purely human viewpoint, or giving in to some desire that leads you away from pleasing the Lord.

2. Cry Out to God

Take your need to Him, knowing you don't have to yield to the power of sin. Memorize and repeat to yourself, "For the power of the life-giving Spirit has freed [me] through Christ Jesus from the power of sin that leads to death" (Rom. 8:2 NLT).

3. Act in God's Power and According to Who You *Now* Are

What are you and I to do when tempted by our old sinful nature? Here are some commands, not suggestions, that God gives: Count yourself dead to sin; don't let sin control your life; don't let any part of your body become a tool of wickedness; throw off your old evil nature and what belongs to your former way of life. Instead, put on the new self created to be like God; set the desires of your heart and the thoughts of your mind on what pleases the Lord; physically and mentally flee whatever could draw you into sin.

You and I can live a life that radiates love for God. By choosing to live under the Spirit's control, you needn't respond to the tugs of your old sinful nature. Depend on God's strength, which is always available through the Spirit, and commit yourself to doing what He commands. Then watch for the incredible changes He will bring about in you.

Daily Choices for the Growing Heart
Depend on God's Strength, Not Your Own

Abraham, Sarah, and Hagar had character flaws that brought a lot of pain and heartache into their world. Ours will too, if we don't turn to God for His help to change. To begin depending on God's strength, not your own:

- Recognize that change happens not in response to willpower, but want-power.

- Depend on God. Forget about grabbing yourself by the scruff of the neck and giving yourself a good talking-to. This is not the same as depending on God; neither is passively waiting for some spiritual cloud to descend and take over for you.

- Humble yourself. Admit to God where you depend on your personality, persuasiveness, or ability to intimidate or manipulate in order to get your way. Perhaps you do this with your spouse or other family member, or someone you're trying to impress or gain power over.

- Commit to changing your responses. Ask God to help you catch yourself whenever you respond to people and situations in your own strength. Take a breath and refocus, choosing to depend on His wisdom, His direction, His will, and then doing what He wants.

- Aim to please God. Trust Him to work in you, providing the want-power to walk under the control of His Spirit.

Nine

Turn Failure into a Learning Experience

***In every event of failure, God has planted
a seed of success.[1]***

"*I* know several women who are close to burnout," said Bonnie, the director of a training program for women in Christian ministry. "They love the Lord and care about people so much that they find it hard to ever say no to requests for help." Bonnie paused, looked out the window, and then said, "What they need to do is schedule time for rest and recuperation in order to keep giving out as they do, but that's hard when so many have hurts and needs."

What Bonnie said reminded me of an article I'd just read about why people work long hours. I told her, "This article claims that one reason for working long hours and experiencing burnout is simply because we like to feel important. I think people often over-commit in Christian ministry not necessarily because they love the Lord but because of their own ego needs and desire to seem special."

At once I felt a freeze descend like an icy curtain between us. Instead of continuing to catch up on our families and ministry, she and I struggled to make conversation. I left our lunch date wondering what had happened.

I didn't have to wait long for the answer. As I was driving home, the Holy Spirit reminded me of what I'd said. Speaking to my heart, He said, "*Poppy, you were judgmental and critical about people you don't even know. You made a blanket statement that not only reflected on Bonnie's friends but also on her husband, who went through burnout because he gave all he had to serve Me. What came out of your mouth was a true videotape of your heart.*" Ugh. I knew the Holy Spirit was right, as always. I felt sick, and ashamed of myself.

Lord, I prayed, *this isn't the kind of person I want to be. I don't want to be harsh and judgmental, but at times I do open my mouth and insert my foot. I wasn't sympathetic or understanding. Besides, I didn't even show appreciation for those who serve you so sacrificially. Lord, I'm sorry. You say that "out of the heart the mouth speaks," and I've proved you right once again. What I said wasn't worthy of you. Oh, please, help me learn and grow from this experience.*

Centuries ago the prophet Jeremiah said, "The human heart is most deceitful and desperately wicked. Who really knows how bad it is?" (Jer. 17:9 NLT). How true. My lack of empathy, my quickness to judge, and my hurtful words spoken without thinking revealed what crouched inside me—and I didn't like what I saw.

More than that, someone I esteem saw the ugly stuff that lay deep within. I didn't like that either. Please understand—I agree in my head with the truth that I'm a sinner. I really have no trouble admitting it in a general sense—but who wants to let other people see you actually sinning? That's embarrassing.

The minute I saw why I was embarrassed, however, I saw all too clearly that pride also belonged on my growing list of sins. What a murky mess lay hidden beneath the warm, friendly person I had assumed I was.

Have you ever gone through something similar? Discovered that you're not without faults? Been deeply sobered by the Spirit's swift conviction? Ever groaned with a heavy sense of failure—you want to be pleasing to the Lord, yet somehow you can't seem to get beyond what trips you up? Does the Enemy whisper, "God's had enough of your failures," and you find yourself thinking he's probably right? Ever called yourself a useless Christian, felt hopeless, and thought that even if God can forgive you, you can't forgive yourself?

- Take a moment and jot down how you react when you realize you've failed God in some way. What do you think? How do you feel? What do you say to yourself?

You're not alone if you struggle on these occasions with depressing thoughts and feelings. All of us who truly desire to walk with God and to be changed from the inside out, find ourselves wrestling from time to time with what we see crouched deep in our hearts. Be glad for your spiritual sensitivity that produces genuine sorrow and repentance, because this not only pleases God, it's essential if times of failure are to give birth to growth. Peter wept when his faith failed and he denied that he knew Jesus. So should we when we disappoint God.

To Fail Is Human

Failure isn't a pleasant topic. Even thinking about it can set ablaze guilt, self-accusation, and depression. Furthermore, awareness of any sin, deliberate or impulsive, offers fertile soil for the Evil One's attacks. Coiling himself around our minds and hearts, Satan, the Father of Lies, hisses: "You didn't just fail, you *are* a failure. You'll never be any different. You'll *always* let God and everyone else down."

Listen to the Enemy, and failure quickly becomes an emotional and spiritual trap. Rather than failure being an opportunity to review honestly where you are in your walk with God, Satan's goading opens the door to powerfully negative self-talk. Instead of focusing on what you can learn from an experience of failure, have you ever heard yourself asking, *How could you have done that? What kind of person are you to act like that? You know better than to say what you did.*

Under this self-inflicted bombardment of blame and disgust, comforting thoughts of God's forgiveness and restoration quickly evaporate. What takes their place? A smothering sense of hopelessness, skepticism, and spiritual indifference. "After all," the deceiver jabs, "why try to become someone you can never be?"

Who's Calling You a Failure?

When you hear negative, accusing messages, pay close attention. God *never* speaks words of discouragement and hopelessness to His own. No matter how badly we might have failed Him, this is not how He treats His children, Amy Carmichael writes, "Do not forget that discouragement is always from beneath; encouragement is always from above; God is the God of Encouragement."[2]

Rather than being shocked at what we're capable of, God isn't surprised when failure happens. He knows what's in us far more than we do. Much as we earnestly wish it weren't so, in our journey toward maturity we *will* fall short of always achieving the perfectly loving, understanding, wise, and humble character of Jesus. Why? Because we are a work in progress. We walk day by day toward the goal of becoming like Jesus, but not one of us has arrived. God knows this and He wants us to know it.

God, who lovingly redeems, restores, and rebuilds the broken places in our lives calls us to face our failures and turn them into profoundly useful learning experiences. "The wise woman builds," writes Solomon. "I press on," declares Paul. "Go on to maturity," urges the writer of Hebrews (Prov. 14:1; Phil. 3:14; Heb. 6:1). Our walk with God is always a call to move forward, to come up higher.

Over the past few years this has been Kay's happy experience. As we talked one day about how God responds to us when we've blown it, she quietly shared her story. "Things weren't going well at home between Bob and me," she confided. "The classic scenario developed at work: I spent too much time with a male colleague. We found ourselves attracted to each other, and one thing led to another. Our affair didn't last long, but guilt devastated me."

Taking a deep breath, Kay added: "I'd been active in our church, even considered a leader among the women, but I wondered if God could ever bear to love me or use me again. I failed horribly, but I'm so glad I knew enough to go back to the Lord on my knees and repent, rather than run even further away from Him."

Kay's painful yet necessary time of confession pulled the plug on Satan's schemes to destroy her relationship with God. Instead of hiding from a guilt-plagued conscience, she now knows firsthand the joy of God's redeeming, restoring, and rebuilding power.

When failure happens, it's appropriate to grieve and be humble before God. Just don't fall into the trap of thinking this is your permanent condition—it isn't. Failure is a temporary experience.

Believe that you *can* move forward with God and that this is not only possible but also is His great joy to work in you to make it happen.

Our heads might assure us that we follow the God of second, third, and however many more chances we need, but how do we shed our feelings of guilt and hopelessness? What is necessary in order to experience the Father's forgiveness no matter how badly we've failed? Is it possible to do something about our vulnerable areas *before* we land on our faces in the mud? God has answers for these important questions.

To find God's answers, let's look at the three necessary components for turning failure into a learning experience. Every time you sin and fall short of what pleases God, and every time the Holy Spirit lovingly shows you where you've gone wrong, ask the Father to help you:

- Deal with guilt
- Delight in God's grace
- Discover where you need to grow

Deal With Guilt

Failure and guilt have been around since the first sin in the Garden of Eden. None of us has escaped their clutches—not even God's friend Abraham. After going along with Sarah's plan, when did the sickening realization grip him: "I've run ahead of God. I took matters into my own hands. I should have waited for His timing— what have I done?"

Was it immediately following his encounter with Hagar? When she became pregnant and treated barren Sarah with contempt? Could it have been after Ishmael was born, and God's silence dragged on year after year? We don't know. Whenever that precise moment came, however, we can be certain that Abraham felt the same sickening jolt of guilt that hits everyone who longs to please God—and realizes she's done just the opposite.

Abraham was eighty-six years old when Hagar bore Ishmael. He was ninety-nine when God appeared to him again, saying, "I am God Almighty; walk before me and be blameless" (Gen. 17:1). These thirteen years must have been an agonizing period of silence, causing Abraham to wonder what had happened to his relationship with his Sovereign Lord.

Would God ever appear to him again? What about all His promises? Abraham must have wondered if he'd totally blown what God wanted to do with his life. Imagine his wrestling, confusion, and deep sense of guilt—thoughts and feelings that perhaps you can identify with, as I can.

God doesn't hide from us the faults and failings of even His greatest saints. His message comes through loud and clear: Every one of us has failed. We've all done things we're ashamed of. And I, for one, sincerely hope there will be no revealing of all my secrets in heaven. Only God needs to know.

Because guilt plagues everyone from time to time, we need to know how to deal with it. To do this, let's first explore some facts about this powerful emotion.

Guilt: A Universal Emotion

Glancing out of our hotel window during a stopover in Singapore several years ago, Jim and I noticed a procession going by. We watched in horror and fascination for a few minutes, and then raced down to the street to get a closer look. What we saw wasn't a political demonstration with people shouting and waving banners—this was a Hindu festival, and the participants were demonstrating their devotion to one of their gods.

Surrounded by friends and family, streams of men marched by, literally skewered with long, thin, metal rods. Some rods went through their top lip, tongue, and bottom lip. Others pierced through one cheek and out the other. Small metal hooks, inserted into their backs and chests, supported elaborate wire cages decorated with feathers and flowers.

What was this festival, called Thaipusam, all about? The participants were celebrating the victory of Lord Murugan, the son of Shiva, over evil. They willingly undergo this incredibly painful ritual in order to express their thanks for blessings received, to try to gain special favors and to *atone for their sins.*

Because guilt is a universal experience, people around the world pay whatever price seems necessary to gain emotional relief or ward off whatever punishment they dread might happen. For some, this includes willingly being pierced with metal rods and hooks. Others offer gifts of food, flowers, or money to the spirits, do acts of penance, or make costly vows of devotion.

For believers in Jesus Christ, none of this is necessary. We don't have to atone for our sin or suffer the pain of skewered flesh *or* skewered emotions when we fail. We've been set free by the atoning death of God's Son.

Doesn't that make you heave a great sigh of relief, clap your hands, or do a little jig? Better still, to fervently thank God? However you respond to this life-liberating truth, rejoice and celebrate, because: "Since we have been made right in God's sight by faith, we have peace with God because of what Jesus Christ our Lord has done for us" (Rom. 5:1 NLT).

Guilt: True and False

"Talk with people who are depressed, lonely, dealing with marriage problems ... or facing almost any other problem, and you will

192

find people who experience guilt as part of their difficulties," writes Dr. Gary Collins, in *Christian Counseling.* "Guilt is so prevalent in our society," he says, "that several types have been identified. These can be divided into two categories; objective guilt and subjective guilt."[3]

Objective Guilt

Objective guilt is the result of breaking a law—*whether we feel guilty about it or not.* This law might be God's divine standard, some earthly law that governs how we live, an unwritten but socially expected code of behavior, or a personal standard that governs our conscience.

Realizing I would be late for church one Sunday morning, I stepped on the gas. Racing through the quiet streets it never occurred to me to check either the speed limit or my rearview mirror. Hurtling around the corner into the church parking lot, I slammed on my brakes, grabbed my Bible, yanked open the door—and found myself nose to nose with a state patrol officer.

"Madam," he intoned, as other churchgoers walked past smiling sympathetically, "you were doing sixty in a thirty-five miles per hour zone." I smiled weakly, hoping for mercy.

Was I objectively guilty of breaking the law? No doubt about it—and not just then but many times since, especially when I get engrossed in a fascinating conversation with myself while driving.

- How about you? Can you think of times when you have been objectively guilty, perhaps when driving or doing something else? Are there some laws—whether divine, governmental, social, or personal—that you struggle to keep? Reflect for a moment and write down what comes to mind.

Subjective Guilt

In contrast to objective guilt, subjective guilt is what makes us *feel* uneasy and miserable about ourselves. Often we can't think of any objective reason for our feelings of guilt, we just know that some situations trigger that reaction. We *feel* guilty—but *are* we, really? And why is it that some things that make *me* feel guilty don't affect *you*, and vice versa? Even stranger, how can we feel guilty for actions or things that God doesn't condemn at all?

My friend Rose, the daughter of missionaries and one herself, confessed, "I feel guilty whenever I sit down to read a magazine. I know there's always more to be done for the Lord. People need to be visited and encouraged; I should be doing more Scripture memorization; I could be sewing for the poor. But the truth is, I'm tired and a quiet hour with a cup of tea and a magazine is so much more appealing."

I'd be tired out myself if I took on even a fraction of Rose's activities. Is Rose breaking some divine law? Should she feel guilty? Unless taking a little rest is violating Scripture, and the Holy Spirit is convicting her, Rose has no reason to condemn herself.

Other people (I'm one of them) feel guilty about not making time to respond to letters. Perhaps you, too, get lots of mail every Christmas, and you vow you'll write back—but the next year rolls around and you realize you still haven't written. Should we feel guilty for breaking this unwritten social rule? Some people will, and some won't. Consider these other potentially guilt-inducing behaviors: splurging more money on a new outfit than you intended, relishing each bite of a luscious dessert, not giving to every charity that has you on a mailing list.

- You may or may not relate to these examples, but take a moment to reflect on what does make you *feel* guilty. Is there a valid reason for your feelings? If not, where do you think they come from?

The list of reasons to feel guilty can be overwhelming, but think about this: Not every twinge of guilt comes from God. See if you recognize these other sources:

- **Childhood conditioning:** Your parents said, "Finish everything on your plate because there are poor, starving children all over the world, and it's wrong to waste food." Now what happens when you, a grown-up, don't eat everything on your plate? You guessed it, you feel guilty.

- **Family patterns:** If you sat around daydreaming, Mom or Dad found work for you to do. The message? Relaxing or doing nothing was declared lazy, bad, wasting your life. Even now you feel guilty when you long to take a break from being Super Mom, dedicated employee, amorous wife, and Martha Stewart rolled into one— every single day.

- **Church teachings:** You know you don't measure up to what the pastor teaches: witness to your friends at work; prayer-walk your neighborhood, interceding for each household; fix a casserole for the sick; and most important, volunteer for nursery duty with all those noisy little two-legged gifts from God. Every time you hear of another way you could serve God, your guilt buttons are pushed and the voice of the Evil One shouts: "You are not what you should be."

Without a doubt, feelings of guilt are shaped and built, in part, by our upbringing and other people's expectations. Thankfully, even though we can't eradicate those influences, we can learn to overcome their ability to rob us of peace and God's joy.

Steps to Peace

1. Ask God to reveal why you feel guilty. Don't wait, wallowing in negative feelings about yourself. Be like David. Ask God to search your heart (Ps. 139:23-24).

2. Use your common sense: analyze whether your feelings have any substance. If they don't, ask God to heal your overactive conscience and help you break free from unbiblical expectations.

3. Reject any thoughts of condemnation or accusation from the Enemy (Rom. 8:1).

4. Use God's Word as your guide for what's right and wrong, being sensitive and alert to the Holy Spirit's voice.

5. Confide in more mature Christians about your quandary, asking for their counsel and prayers.

What should we do, though, when we *have* violated God's standards?

Instead of self-condemnation, which is Satan's misery-making strategy, God calls us to constructive sorrow. Writing to the Corinthians, Paul says, "Your sorrow led you to repentance. For you became sorrowful as God intended.... Godly sorrow brings repentance.... See what this godly sorrow has produced in you" (2 Cor. 7:9-11).

Godly sorrow is *not* the same as feeling ashamed of ourselves. We can feel down or embarrassed because we've lost someone's respect, our mask of perfection has slipped, or we don't like the consequences of what we've done. All of these responses focus on *self*. In contrast, godly sorrow is focused on the One we've grieved or offended.

Sorrow for sin becomes constructive when we move from feeling ashamed of ourselves to actively repenting for what we've done. Repentance is saying to God in total sincerity, "I don't want to behave like this again or be this kind of person. Show me how to become who you want me to be." This kind of seriousness with God not only softens ours hearts, it lays the foundation for turning failure into a learning experience.

Once your heart is softened, follow God's path to freedom as found in 1 John 1:7-10:

1. Confess your failure to God. Refuse to minimize, excuse, or pretend. Instead, humbly acknowledge what happened and agree with God that you sinned.

2. Thank God for the fact that Christ died for this specific sin. "The blood of Jesus, his Son, purifies us from *all* sin."

3. Confess, if your heart tells you this is necessary, to those affected by your wrongdoing, and make restitution as needed.

4. Work at cultivating an attitude of grace and respect toward yourself. You have been forgiven and God wants you to grow. Make this, not the past, your focus.

Hard as it is to fathom, God yearns for us to come to Him whenever we fail. He will never push us away because of our human weakness. Listen, and then let yourself believe and respond to these great words of hope: "'Come now, let us reason together,' says the Lord. 'Though your sins are like scarlet, they shall be as white as snow; though they are red as crimson, they shall be like wool'" (Isa. 1:18).

Delight in God's Grace

Embedded in the heart of the Gospel is the amazing truth that God does *not* deal with us according to what we deserve. Instead, He invites us to rejoice like little children, splashing around with sheer delight in the ever-flowing fountain of His grace—His undeserved, unearned, life-transforming love and acceptance that He so lavishly pours upon us.

Abraham tasted this truth when God finally broke His long, thirteen-year silence, revealing himself not only as God Almighty, El Shaddai, but also as the God of grace. During the years of silence, Abraham might well have wondered where God was, yearning for a fresh encounter with Him—just as we do when we haven't sensed His presence for some time. But God hadn't turned His back on Abraham for taking matters into his own hands. Nor had He put him on the shelf, choosing to transfer His promises to some more worthy person, as we can fear is the case with us.

No, when God saw that Abraham was finally ready for what He planned to do, He strode into His servant's life with a fresh revelation of himself and His purposes. Making a clear reference to Abraham's less-than-faith-directed behavior with Hagar, God commanded, "Walk before me and be blameless" (Gen. 17:1).

Here is God's grace in action. In spite of all Abraham had done—rushing ahead of God, neglecting to wait and discover His will, creating pain and discord in his household—this imperfect man didn't hear God call him a weak, useless failure. Unexpectedly, He commanded Abraham to come up higher, to look forward. From now on he was not to live like the people around him, always trying to find clever solutions to his problems. He must live by faith alone, trusting God to show him what to do. "Walk before *me*, Abraham, not before other people's opinions, demands, or ideas" was His message. Only in this way could Abraham walk worthy of his stupendous, scary, impossible calling.

God's grace-filled message to Abraham after he failed was not to him alone; it also applies to you and me. No matter how great a mess we've made, God still says, "Look ahead. Today holds the seed of your new beginning. Walk before *me*. Keep your faith fixed on *me*. Live worthy of your calling to follow *me*."

During the years I taught a Bible Study Fellowship class, one of my joys was choosing the hymns we sang. A favorite that still stirs my soul goes,

Marvelous, infinite, matchless grace,

Freely bestowed on all who believe!

You that are longing to see His face,

Will you this moment His grace receive?[4]

As recipients of His marvelous grace "that will pardon and cleanse within," our every failure becomes an opportunity for transformation, not a one-way ticket to a spiritual dead end.

"Because of the Lord's great love we are not consumed, for his compassions never fail. They are new every morning; great is your faithfulness," declared Jeremiah, as he wept at the consequences Israel suffered because of her sin (Lam. 3:22-23). Hope for a fresh beginning—whether for Abraham, Israel, or for us—is always rooted in the unchanging grace and love of God.

Kristin's story illustrates this wonderful truth. A married forty-something nurse, Kristin said defiantly, "My friend pressured me into coming to this retreat and told me I needed to talk to you. I don't know why I'm here, because there's nothing wrong with my life. I have a good marriage, great kids, I like my job—I'm just fine."

After asking Kristin to tell me more about herself, I soon discovered that her story had a bizarre twist.

"I've been praying that God would bring my old high-school sweetheart back into my life," she confided, "and He has. In fact, we're going to meet soon for a weekend together."

Incredulous, I asked, "You believe God answered your prayer?" She nodded, smiling. However, when I pointed out that God doesn't help us to sin, her smile quickly vanished.

Somehow, though, we stayed in close touch over the next few months. My concern for Kristin grew as her distorted thinking dragged her down into a suicidal depression. Ultimately she was admitted to an inpatient Christian mental-health facility. After weeks of intensive treatment followed by two years of therapy, Kristin learned the importance of examining and questioning her thoughts and assumptions, looking for what was true and discarding the lies that swirled around in her mind.

Today Kristin shares her faith, helps organize women's conferences, and actively supports other Christians struggling with life issues. "I was walking away from everything I believed and valued," she told me years later. "I'm amazed that God would forgive me and straighten out the mess I was making of my life. He turned me around from being spiritually deceived and angry at Him for stopping me from having an affair. I'm so grateful."

Every time I think of the change God's grace has made in Kristin's life, I smile with delight.

- As you look back over your walk with God, where have you experienced His amazing grace? What has He forgiven you of? How has He changed you? Take a few moments to reflect, writing to God your words of gratitude or praise.

Discover Where You Need to Grow

The command "Walk before me and be blameless," given to Abraham and to us as followers of Christ, does not imply that we can achieve a state of sinlessness while on earth. For that to happen, we'd have to become like God, utterly holy and eternally perfect, without flaw or failing. No, being blameless or perfect means to practice living out in our character and conduct what we say we believe. We are to aim at being completely what we claim: entirely sincere, full of integrity, consistent both outwardly and inwardly with our calling to live consciously before God day by day.

Much as we genuinely yearn to live like this, the truth is we all fail from time to time. What a waste, then, if we don't learn all we can from our failures by being honest with God and ourselves. Emphasizing this truth, Dr. Charles Stanley counsels, "Glean a lesson from your failures, but don't frame them and hang them on the wall of your emotions for constant viewing."[5]

Acknowledging what we did wrong and delighting in God's grace is fundamental. But we must go deeper. To gain spiritual wisdom we need to identify our weaknesses, fearlessly probe what led to our experience of failure, and then erect safeguards to help us prevent recurrence. "The wisdom of the prudent," says Solomon, "is to *give thought* to their ways" (Prov. 14:8). To glean a lesson from failure, focus your thoughts on the following:

Acknowledge Your Vulnerability

During World War II, British and Australian troops prepared to defend the tiny island of Singapore. Nestled under the Malaysian peninsula, Singapore lay vulnerable to the threat of air and sea attack by the Japanese. Because the Allied forces believed the battle would come on the more exposed side of the island, they massed their men and supplies there, confidently pointing all their antiaircraft guns outward, toward the sea. Too late, the Allied troops discovered the Japanese had swept down through Malaysia itself, crossing into Singapore where they least expected it. After a short, furious battle, the Allied troops surrendered, and the Japanese declared victory.

In order to experience spiritual victory instead of defeat, we, too, must discover where we're vulnerable. The pride and overconfidence that assumes the Enemy could never have a victory in our lives leaves us as unprepared for attack as those forces in Singapore. By humbly acknowledging we're not above falling, even in areas where we think we're strong, we're more likely to be self-aware, vigilant, and victorious. "If you think you are standing firm, be careful that you don't fall!" warns Paul (1 Cor. 10:12).

Analyze Possible Contributing Factors

To protect yourself from attitudes or actions that conflict with your heart's desire to please the Lord, pray for insight into *where* you're vulnerable, then brace yourself for the truth. Could it be lying, like Abraham? Having a quick fuse, like Sarah? Being haughty and proud, like Hagar? Greedy and self-seeking, like Lot? The list goes on and on: being supersensitive, wallowing in self-pity, getting pleasure from passing on tidbits of gossip that don't edify anyone, being judgmental and quick to find fault. None of us can claim to be above the possibility of these behaviors—we're all vulnerable.

Ask the Spirit to help you probe fearlessly beneath the surface, to tap into how you tick, to recognize the various factors that trip you up.

When You're Tempted to Lie

Ask: Do I feel pressured to impress others? To gain advantage over a perceived rival? To cover up something I lack the courage to admit?

When Your Problem Is Ungodly Anger

Ask: Do I blow a fuse under pressure when the kids demand my help *now*, my husband can't find the checkbook, everyone is waiting for me to hurry and get dinner on the table? Am I angry with myself for being disorganized, angry with others for not helping, or reacting to something someone said or did earlier that day?

When You Struggle with Pride

Ask: Why do I feel I have greater ability than others to handle a task? That I, after all, know best? That those I work or serve with should just listen to me and do what I advise? Probe some more, asking: Why am I hungry to feel superior to others? What fears or unmet needs push me to feel this way?

When You're Tempted Morally

Ask: What's going on? Have I opened a door for the Enemy to sweep into my life by acting on my curiosity about the unknown or forbidden? Have I allowed an assault on my soul by joining in sexually explicit conversations at work, reading steamy novels, watching certain television talk shows, movies, or cable channels that at first shocked me, but now have me addicted? Has hunger for God been destroyed by my lack of vigilance, just as the Allied troops on Singapore were destroyed because they failed to recognize the danger they were in?

These illustrations show only a few of the many ways each of us is vulnerable to spiritual and moral failure. Whatever your particular weakness, ask God to open your eyes to what's going on in you. What pulls at you from within? What lowers your defenses? Is there an attitude, a mood, a lack of discipline, an unrepentant heart, or spiritual dryness that triggers your vulnerability?

- Take a few minutes to reflect on these questions, then record whatever God shows you.

Activate Your Defenses

Our spiritual defense systems need to be put in place *before* we're attacked. That we will be attacked is a given. That we will fail need not be so. Much depends on the preventative action we take on a regular basis. Unlike the troops in Singapore whose resources were inadequate to defend the island and were wrongly used, God's provision will prove totally sufficient for the battles we face. Let's look at what these are and how we activate them:

Intimacy With God

Time to read the Word, listen, think, and journal is vital. Someone has said, "An army advances on its stomach." A starving soldier has little strength for battle. The same is spiritually true of us. Without regular feeding on the Word, we gradually get weaker and weaker. Then, when the Enemy attacks, we're knocked flat faster than we dreamed possible.

If you can, get into a class or small group where you're taught the Word. Make it a priority in your week. If that's not possible, work through a Bible study book on your own. Or read a segment of Scripture, pray for insight, and write down what you think God is saying and how He wants you to apply it to your life that day.

When you study Scripture, take time to pray back to God what you've read. If the passage praises Him—pray it back, adding your own thoughts. If some sin is mentioned, confess your own. If there's a promise, see what it's saying about God's character and claim that for yourself. If there's a command, ponder how you're keeping it or what action you need to take. Turn whatever you read in the Bible into reasons for prayer. Keep a list of what you're thankful for; keep adding to it. Pray for your family, friends, people you know—let your heart be filled with their needs and concerns and your prayers won't remain focused only on you.

In addition to making time for Scripture and prayer, invest in good devotional books to read every day. These expand your sensitivity to God, as will other helpful books your pastor, teacher, or friends might recommend.

Involvement With Others

Another important element in building a spiritual defense system is spending time with people who share your desire to walk closely with the Lord. We all need the input of those who inspire and encourage us to stay faithful to our calling. We need someone who will phone or make contact deliberately to ask how we're doing—not because she's a busybody, but because she cares.

Appearing spiritual on the outside, yet knowing ourselves to be quite different in the privacy of our homes or our minds, is fatally easy. Covering up the truth and refusing to face facts about our behavior or ourselves happens when no one asks the hard questions.

In his sensitive book on spiritual and moral failure, *Rebuilding Your Broken World*, Pastor Gordon MacDonald lists twenty-six questions to ask friends, and to have them ask you. Here are a few examples, but be sure you and your friend first give each other permission to use them.

"How is your relationship with God right now?"

"What have you read in the Bible in the past week?"

"What has God said to you in this reading?"

"What specific things are you praying for in regard to yourself?"

"How are you doing with your spouse? Kids?"

"Are there any unresolved conflicts in your circle of relationships right now?"[6]

A friend once confided, "I'm hungry for someone to talk 'Jesus talk' with me." Do you have anyone like that? Are you that kind of friend—one who helps build the spiritual defense system of another?

Investment in Others' Lives

The writer of Hebrews urges believers to "consider how we may spur one another on toward love and good deeds" (Heb. 10:24). This takes time and thought, but above all, requires a willingness to invest in others because you care about their well-being.

In building your spiritual defense system, recognize the strengthening power of being invested in someone else's life. Not only are you a blessing to that person but she also looks at you with respect, counts on you as one who is growing in Christ, and helps you to stay strong because of your commitment to her. Studies show that we are all more inclined to live up to other people's expectations than to our own. In this case, investing in others offers a double return: to the person you encourage, and to yourself.

- As you reflect on where you need to grow in order to avoid failure, what steps do you need to take in the following areas to activate your spiritual defense system?

- Intimacy with God:

- Involvement with others:

- Investment in others' lives:

After calling Abraham to walk before Him and be blameless, God repeated the glorious promises He had given years before: "Abraham, you *will* have a son, you *will* be a father of many nations, you *will* become very fruitful, the whole land of Canaan *will* be yours—and *Sarah will be the mother of your promised child*" (Gen. 17:3-16, author's paraphrase).

Refusing to leave Abraham with the permanently sour taste of failure in his mouth, God poured out His lavish grace on His imperfect yet maturing servant. In response, Abraham fell facedown before the Lord, overwhelmed at the wonder of His undeserved blessings.

Can we, who have received God's amazing grace, who also struggle with guilt, and who know we need to always keep growing, do any less?

Daily Choices for the Growing Heart
Turn Failure Into a Learning Experience

Failure has been described as the back door to success. For this to be your experience:

- Recognize the opportunity in failure—view it as God's invitation to come close and receive mercy and grace.

- Look for the growth lessons it contains—let your experience of failure produce necessary changes in your attitude or behavior.

- Don't waste what you've learned—apply the lessons that failure teaches.

- Refuse to let an occasion of failure hold you down—instead, let it propel you toward becoming more like Christ.

Ten

Live to Hear God's "Well Done"

***The greatest concern of life is to place our relationship
with God first, and everything else second.[1]***

"Eric, don't move. There's a tarantula by your foot," Roxie whispered
urgently.

Having shut off the electric generator for the night, Eric, a
missionary to Mexico, sat in the living room trying to read by the
light of a single candle. Roxie, his wife, had been reading in their tiny
bedroom when suddenly she felt prompted to go into the living room.
What she saw made her freeze.

Eric stiffened in response to her warning, his bare feet within
easy striking distance of the huge venomous spider. Looking up, he
sat motionless, watching as Roxie slowly and quietly slid toward the
kitchen, returning in a moment with a large jar. Creeping cautiously,
she slammed it down with one swift movement, trapping the biggest
tarantula either of them had seen in their twelve years of living in
Mexico.

Living to hear God's "well done" often leads to living on the edge. In the case of our friends Eric and Roxie, "the edge" is the Mexican jungle, lying just a few feet from where they live half the year. Passionate about Jesus Christ and wanting to hear His "well done" regardless of the cost, they cheerfully make their home in a few small rooms at a rural Mexican Bible school.

"Sharing in the lives of our students is well worth any 'sacrifices' involved," writes Roxie. "We're learning it's not so bad having electricity for just a couple of hours at night, or living without hot running water. We're also delighting in the little pleasures God drops our way, even uninvited guests in the form of unwanted creepy crawlies."

After three months of intensive Bible teaching each fall, the Mexican students return to their villages to share what they've learned. But instead of being welcomed, they sometimes experience rejection and violence. Knowing this, each spring Eric and Roxie travel hundreds of miles to visit them, driving on dirt roads in remote areas. For several months their small camper van is home, office, and transportation, allowing them to stop for a day or two to encourage, advise, and pray with the young men and women they've grown to love.

Are Eric and Roxie young, fearless risk takers? Hardly. They have grandchildren, aging parents, and little financial security. Of course, they could live less risky lives if they chose to—but they don't. They began walking with God many years ago, and as far as they are concerned, every day is a new spiritual adventure. Plans to quit and take life easy don't even enter their minds, because their passion is to live lives that focus on finishing well. That is their goal.

When I think about people who live to hear God's "well done," Eric and Roxie always come to mind. They don't grit their teeth, resigning themselves to living sacrificially. Nor do they count the days till they can get back to a more "normal" life. This sometimes dangerous place is where they want to be; this is where they are blessed from head to toe; this is where they invest their lives daily, gladly, for God's glory.

What about you? Do you know someone with a similar passion—not necessarily a missionary or an impossibly perfect super-saint—perhaps a friend whose life affects yours because of her single-minded eagerness to please God? You're fortunate if you do. More important, God wants *you* to become that kind of person.

When Jesus said, "Seek first His [God's] kingdom"; "Whoever loses his life for my sake will find it"; and "If anyone would come after me, he must deny himself and take up his cross and follow me," He was calling us to single-minded devotion to himself (Matt. 6:33; 10:39; 16:24). He makes it clear that if we want to be His disciples, our pursuit of God must be both passionate and intentional. Living to hear His "well done" is a choice we make. It doesn't happen automatically.

Choosing to Live for God

Nothing gets accomplished in life without our making choices. We don't graduate from college, lose weight, play the piano, run a marathon, or overcome a disability without making the choice to do so. The same is true if we yearn to hear God's "well done."

Left to ourselves, few of us would live in conscious pursuit of God. Even as Christians, our human inclination always gravitates to the easy choices, the less costly way. "From silken self, O Captain, free Thy soldier who would follow Thee," prayed Amy Carmichael of India many years ago. Today, Tony Campolo warns, "The greatest danger to those who would follow Jesus is not overt persecution from society, but subtle seduction by its values."[2]

In the parable of the talents, Jesus describes three servants whose master gave each of them a certain amount of money. He expected these servants to wisely invest what was entrusted to them. Two out of the three recognized the privilege and opportunity given to them and did what their master asked. One did not. Two heard their master's "well done." One did not.

What made the difference? Two valued all they had been given and, as a result, chose to invest their treasure because they wanted to please their master. One chose not to make the effort (Matt. 25:14-27).

God has entrusted opportunities, blessings, and gifts to you and to me. He has lavishly provided us with everything for our enjoyment. And because all we have and are belong to Him first, we're commanded to "do good, to be rich in good deeds, generous and willing to share" (1 Tim. 6:17-19). God doesn't give us His Spirit and blessings so we can live as the center of our own private universe. His purposes for your life and mine are far greater than that.

Pursuing God's vision for our lives demands purpose-oriented living. The apostle Paul, fervently desiring to strengthen believers, stresses this truth repeatedly: "Each one should be careful how he builds"; "Be very careful, then, how you live"; "Train yourself to be godly.... Be diligent in these matters; give yourself wholly to them" (1 Cor. 3:10; Eph. 5:15; 1 Tim. 4:7, 15).

Declaring that nothing in his life compared with the thrill of knowing Christ, Paul powerfully expressed his longing to *know Him more*, to *be like Him*, and to *live fully and completely for Him*. Paul's longings didn't stop with wishful thinking or spine-tingling daydreams. He made intentional choices. "I press on," he declared firmly. Why? What goal demanded his wholehearted, lifelong determination and effort? The desire to make a name for himself? To have people admire him? No. What drove Paul was "to take hold of that for which Christ Jesus took hold of me" (Phil. 3:12).

Paul knew, from his life-changing encounter with the living Christ, what he was to do with his life and how he was to live. His overwhelming gratitude to the Lord for dying on the cross, plus his acute awareness of God's reality and power, fueled his passion to devote his life to sharing the Gospel.

Paul marveled that Christ would die for him, felt awed by God's magnificence, and became humbly aware that everything he accomplished happened through God's mercy. No wonder he wrote, "Oh, the depth of the riches of the wisdom and knowledge of God! How unsearchable his judgments, and his paths beyond tracing out!" (Rom. 11:33).

- As you reflect on what you've read, ask yourself, *What am I passionate about? What do I want my life to count for? What choices do I need to make in order to live intentionally for God?* Why not write a note to God expressing your heart's response.

"Follow Me, and I Will Make You ..."

When God called Abraham to follow Him, He had a plan in mind for his life. This plan extended beyond any task He might want Abraham to carry out. God intended to change Abraham from the inside out into a man who would love His Creator so much he'd follow Him no matter the cost.

To bring about what He was seeking to produce in Abraham, God fashioned the timing, the life-shaping events, and the kinds of experiences needed. Step by step, He molded Abraham's character, values, attitudes, and behavior. The depth of Abraham's love for God and his spiritual maturity in the greatest test of his life powerfully affirm what God is able to do in a life fully surrendered to Him.

God's inner shaping work is not limited to certain extraordinary people. He makes spiritual giants out of average stuff. Jesus demonstrated this when He chose His disciples. He looked beyond what they were, to *who they would become* as they walked with Him.

When Jesus said, "Follow me, and *I will make you* fishers of men," He issued an invitation to know Him closely, to learn, observe, and be inwardly changed. This call was far more than a summons to join a work crew. Yes, the task of spreading the Gospel occupied the Lord's mind, but setting afire in this motley group a passionate belief, trust, and devotion to Him took first place.

God's training program for those who follow Him today is the same. He is under no illusions about the raw material He has to work with. With insight possible only to Him, He sees what needs to be dug out, faced, and changed in our attitudes and values. He knows our beliefs, behaviors, and instinctive determination to run our own lives and to have our own way.

Yet God clearly sees our potential for spiritual maturity—the ability to think, do, and desire what is pleasing to Him. He knows what we can become when we cooperate with His shaping process, surrendering our often-stubborn heart and will to Him as fully as we know how.

Although the Lord has different tasks for each of us to accomplish, His goal of changing us from the inside out is the same. If we look at the pieces of our lives and try to fit together the broken places, rough edges, and empty holes, we see only a confusing puzzle. Even so,

God is working all these things together, using them to bring about His ultimate purpose: inner change, maturity, and another life yielded and available to Him.

Abraham's response to God throughout his spiritual journey vividly illustrates this. From his initial act of tremendous faith, Abraham sought to steadily pursue his relationship with God. Sure, he had failures, but no failure was fatal or final. His heart never grew cold and his focus never wavered, even as the years passed. In contrast to many whose zeal for the Lord wanes over time, Abraham kept on listening and responding to the living God. He wanted his life to count, he wanted to finish well, he wanted to hear God's "well done." Little wonder his name is revered to this day.

Watch for God at Work

God worked slowly but deeply to transform Abraham, shaping and forming him day by day for many years. This is what God does. He *has* been doing this, and *is* doing it today, in your life and mine. Perhaps you need this reassurance, as Laurie did when her chaotic world finally fell apart.

Finding the courage to leave her abusive, alcoholic husband left Laurie emotionally exhausted. A few days after she had finally called the police for help, she sat nervously with a small group of Christian women—her face drained of color, dark circles outlining her eyes, and hands trembling. By the time she left them that morning, she'd received many reassurances that God was at work in her life for her good.

When Laurie kept anxiously asking about the time, one group member took off her watch and gave it to her. In escaping her home, she had left her watch behind and now feared being late to her new job. Protesting, "I'm not used to taking something from others,"

Laurie heard another woman quickly retort, "Yes, you are. You're used to taking whatever is negative and abusive." That truth struck home not only with Laurie but also with everyone in the group.

God *had* been at work in Laurie's life: He helped her recognize she must escape the danger she was in, and then led her to a church where people showed personal concern. He *continued* to work by surrounding her with women who cared, met a practical need, and offered ongoing support. In the same way God is working to transform Laurie and draw her closer to Him, so He worked in Abraham and continues to work in us.

The ultimate revelation of Abraham's changed character, faith, and passion for God is recorded in the most shocking, awe-inspiring, and powerful event found in the Old Testament. Abraham's positive response to God's command to sacrifice Isaac revealed to both heaven and earth the mighty work God had done in this great man of faith (Gen. 22).

In our final look at this spiritual giant, we see Abraham's mature faith shining through. His response when God tested him to the core of his being not only takes our breath away, it provides us with a vivid example of a life lived totally for God. This incident is full of lessons for us and provokes two questions:

- What shaping tools should we expect *God* to use in developing our faith?

- What is required of *us* in order to keep growing spiritually stronger?

Let's look for answers in the account of Abraham's offering up Isaac.

Expect God to Keep Working in You

Twenty-five years after Abraham began his journey with God and received the initial promise of a son, Isaac was born. The humanly impossible had happened. Imagine the joy, tears, laughter, and sheer exhilaration Abraham and Sarah felt as they looked with wonder on this, their child, born to them despite their age. "By faith," writes the author of Hebrews, whose awe almost jumps off the page, "Abraham, even though he was past age—and Sarah herself was barren—was enabled to become a father because he considered him faithful who had made the promise" (Heb. 11:11).

After Isaac's birth, Abraham probably thought he'd spend the rest of his life enjoying his blessings. We can easily picture the deep bond between a proud father and his beloved son as they walked together, talked around the campfire, and as Abraham taught Isaac what it meant to be a man. Throughout their time together, Abraham must have told Isaac over and over about the one true God and His mighty promises, one of which included his miraculous birth. The love Abraham felt for his son, and the joy and gratitude to God flooding his soul, must have been beyond expression. What more could he possibly desire?

Yet, even though Abraham had totally believed God's promise despite all evidence to the contrary, and ultimately received the son he longed for, God hadn't finished working in his life. Unknown to Abraham, the greatest test and display of his faith and love still lay ahead.

"God, What Are You Doing?"

If you've ever cried out to God, asking this question in confusion and agony, know that you have lots of company. Abraham, the friend of God, certainly knew the pain.

With no warning, and seemingly no reason, Genesis 22 opens with the stark words, "Some time later God tested Abraham." What God said must have sent Abraham reeling. Could he have heard right? Did God really say, "Take your son, the one you love so deeply, and offer him up as a human sacrifice"?

What was God thinking? Other nations practiced human sacrifice, but surely the God who had led him, protected him, and delivered on His promise of a son would not ask for anything so terrible.

This story can make our blood run cold, but it's important to remember that never before, and never again, would God give such an order. God purposely chose this way of testing the depth of Abraham's love and faith. By putting His finger on this most sensitive and vulnerable area of Abraham's life, God forced him to weigh who mattered most to him. Was it his son—or God? The gift or the Giver? Would Abraham's faith in God's promise that through Isaac his descendants would be "as numerous as the stars in the sky or the dust of the earth" stand firm through this test?

God Works Through Testings

If you are serious about walking with God, be prepared for Him to work in your life. In bringing us to greater maturity, God allows various kinds of trials and testings. Tests of our faith, trials that hurt, times of waiting for change to occur, even crushing disappointments can be some of the tools God uses. None of these hard experiences is vengeful punishment hurled down by some cruel divine being.

When we face hard times, we can instinctively, but wrongly, feel we're being unfairly punished by God for some unknown reason. The temptation to question and doubt His love or goodness can overwhelm us. After all, our human reasoning tells us, if God loves me and He is good, surely He wouldn't allow whatever is causing my pain. Actually, God has a track record of using trials and testings. In His wisdom, He does this both to develop our faith and to reveal the depth of our faith. Consider these examples:

- Was God punishing Abraham in this test of faith? No.

- Was God punishing Joseph when he was sold, falsely accused, and imprisoned? No.

- Was God punishing Job when He gave Satan permission to test him? No.

- Was God punishing David when he was hunted like an animal for years? No.

These trials were not meant to torment. Nor are yours or mine. God understands we all need to develop spiritual muscles—which grow strong only through exercise. Think about it from God's perspective: How could we learn that He is there for us and we can depend on Him, if we have no needs? How would we learn that we can persevere by leaning on His strength if our trials disappeared as soon as we prayed about them? How could we learn that God can be trusted with our lives, unless we are faced with circumstances over which we have no control? How would we learn the deep joy that results from obedience, unless God asks it of us?

Development of a solid faith and a deeper relationship with God simply doesn't happen without testings of one kind or another. Hard as they are to go through, they do have positive outcomes when responded to with faith:

Tests Prove What You Believe

When your world comes crashing in, you discover whether what you thought you believed is true or not. Tests reveal your confidence, or lack of confidence, in God's love, His power to provide, and whether you truly believe He is good, regardless of the circumstances.

219

Tests also prove where you're strong and can withstand temptation, or where you're weak and need growth. They reveal whose will you follow—your own or God's. Satan wants you to fail, not trust God, worry, grow bitter, and to carry grudges. The tests God permits, however, are opportunities to hand the Enemy a defeat and, instead, strengthen your commitment to living for God's "well done."

Tests Purify Your Heart

Some tests are like a mirror, reflecting back what is hidden deep within. You might think you love everyone, but when you're tested by having your feathers ruffled, and you can't get your way, what comes out of your heart and spirit? Tolerance, meekness, and a forgiving spirit? Or bitterness, hurt pride, and a desire to get even? Without these tests, none of us would know what needs to be cleaned out of our hearts or brought before God for His help to overcome.

Tests Push You to Higher Levels of Faith

You can either crumble when tests come along—grow angry with God or be overcome with hopelessness—or you can firmly hold on to what you know about Him and claim it for your situation.

In tough times, tests may push you into the Word, searching for some wisdom, a hidden promise, a new direction, or a well-known truth to cling to. Prayer then becomes your power line to peace, your source of comfort and inner stability. Others see you trusting God and are impacted by your faith.

When life is going oh-so-smoothly, spiritual muscles can get pretty flabby. James understood this when he startled people by saying, "Dear brothers and sisters, whenever trouble comes your way, let it be an opportunity for joy. For when your faith is tested, your endurance has a chance to grow. So let it grow, for when your endurance is fully developed, you will be strong in character and ready for anything"

(James 1:2-4 NLT). In God's hands, and responded to with faith and trust, tests and trials push you to new levels of spiritual strength.

- As you look at some of the trials and testings you've experienced, which caused you the greatest spiritual struggle? What are you struggling with today?

- If you could list four positive results of going through hard times depending on God, what would they be?

- How can remembering these help you when another test comes into your life?

God Works Through Living Sacrifices

What does God want from your life and mine? Human sacrifice? No! Never. What He does require is for us to offer ourselves as *living* sacrifices. Paul urges, "I appeal to you therefore, brethren, *and* beg of you in view of the mercies of God, to make a decisive dedication of your bodies—presenting all your members and faculties—as a living sacrifice, holy (devoted, consecrated) and well pleasing to God, which is your reasonable (rational, intelligent) service *and* spiritual worship" (Rom. 12:1 AMP). That truly lays it out, doesn't it?

Paul's passionate appeal to offer ourselves as living sacrifices is based on all we have received from God. Because of His mercy, we have eternal deliverance from God's wrath against sin, unconditional love and acceptance, a life purpose, a new perspective, and the indwelling power of the Holy Spirit, who can change our lives by changing us. In view of this all-encompassing gift, Paul challenges every Christian to make an unshakable decision to serve God fully from the heart. Living to please Him rather than ourselves and sacrificing our wishes if they conflict with His is not only a rational response but also reveals who we worship.

What does a living sacrifice look like? Spend some time reflecting on Jesus' life and you'll find out.

Jesus—Our Supreme Example

The four gospels detail the words, attitudes, and behavior of the Lord. We see His passion to do the Father's will and to finish the work entrusted to Him. He didn't seek to please himself. Rather, He always chose to please the One who sent Him. Because of this, at the end of His life Jesus could say to His Father, "I have brought you glory on earth by completing the work You gave me to do" (John 4:34; 5:30; 17:4).

Nothing could draw Jesus away from His mission on earth. Whether facing applause and popularity, or ridicule, false accusations, and a growing threat of danger and death, He steadfastly continued doing the Father's will.

Jesus, the Messiah, knew who He was. He knew why He was here, and He knew that His work would not be in vain. Even though He shrank in horror from the cup He was to drink, doing the Father's will mattered more to Him than choosing the easier path. Knowing what lay ahead, He could still say, "My Father, if it is possible, may this cup be taken from me. Yet not as I will, but as you will" (Matt. 26:39). In the greatest test a human being ever faced, Jesus surrendered His life to the one He loved more than life itself.

You and I will never be called upon to remotely approach the sufferings of Christ—or to be asked, like Abraham, to kill and sacrifice our own child. Still, God is at work in us to produce a level of devotion that delights to put Him first, a level of trust that confidently holds to His love in life's darkest moments, and a level of surrender that desires only *His* plan for our lives.

Is it possible for a human being to live like this? Abraham demonstrated that it is. So do countless others around the world who live to hear God's "well done."

Take a few moments to think about your own level of devotion, trust, and surrender to God. What evidence of being a living sacrifice do you see expressed in your life? Is something keeping you from living fully for God? Perhaps writing out your thoughts will help.

Abraham was human just like we are. He had to grow in his devotion, trust, and surrender to God just as we do. When God tested Abraham, like metal being tested to reveal its strength, He knew the depth of this man's love, just as He knows the depth of our love. But was Abraham aware of that depth? Are we?

Much of our spiritual formation happens without our realizing it. Sometimes we may think our belief in God is stronger than it actually is. Other times we fail to recognize how deeply we trust Him. Our reaction in times of testing proves what God *has* worked in us, or where we need more spiritual growth.

Requirements to Keep Growing Stronger

Maturing to the point of single-mindedly living to please God is not something that happens without our active cooperation. God expects us to work with Him as He changes us from the inside out. Not surprisingly, Abraham once again models this truth, showing us what is required to walk with God and finish well. Here are three last principles from his life that open the door to our continued growth.

Keep Listening to God's Voice

When Abraham heard God calling his name once again, he answered with eagerness, "Here I am" (Gen. 22:1). Although he didn't know what he would hear, his very attitude at the outset of this great saga of faith teaches us an all-important lesson for our daily walk.

Abraham heard God's voice *because he stayed spiritually alert and eager for any encounter with the One he revered and loved.* With Abraham's open and receptive attitude, God could speak to him knowing Abraham would hear His voice.

Given his circumstances, however, it would have been easy for Abraham to slip into a state of spiritual dullness and become hard-of-hearing. After all, God didn't speak to him very often, he couldn't refresh his memory with any written revelation, and his life was sailing along incredibly well—all conditions that often contribute to tuning out spiritually.

Fuller Seminary professor Dr. Robert Clinton studies the lives of Christian leaders. His extensive research shows why many fail to finish well. In addition to falling into sexual sin, family strife, and pride, he points to "spiritual plateauing" as a major cause.[3] This can happen to any of us if we lose our appetite to know God more deeply.

When Jesus fed the 5,000, John writes that they were given "as much as they wanted" (John 6:11). That comment conjures up pictures in my mind of men patting their full stomachs, stretching out on the grass, and taking a leisurely snooze. The danger is, sometimes we do this spiritually. When we've had plenty of soul food and no longer feel hungry for fresh input from God, we can get spiritually lethargic. Drift along. Hit a plateau, content to stay where we are.

How can you tell if this is happening to you? Check out the following:

- Your time of taking in, chewing over, and digesting God's Word is shrinking.

- You no longer pray consistently or expectantly.

- You no longer notice or expect to see evidences of God at work in your life.

- You are no longer listening for and applying what God says to you personally.

Sense any signs of plateauing? If you do, beware. This isn't what God wants. He knows that living to please Him and finishing well requires an active focus on developing and maintaining a vibrant relationship with Christ. Without that, we'll miss out on all He has planned for us. Abraham never let himself slip into a plateau mode—he stayed tuned in to God's voice. Because of this, God could continue to speak to Abraham's heart and direct his life, pouring out His blessings. He wants to do the same for us.

Keep Responding to What God Says

Commenting on what it means to follow God, one well-known Christian leader states, "The Christian life begins with obedience, depends on obedience, and results in obedience. We can't escape it. The orders from our commander in chief are plain: 'Whoever has my commandments and obeys them, he (she) is the one who loves me' (John 14:21)."

Commitment to God cannot be measured by words or feelings alone. The depth of our love and faith is seen only by our prompt obedience to what He has clearly asked.

When Abraham heard God's command about Isaac, what was required of him became excruciatingly clear. The first impact on this old man's mind must have been one of horror, confusion, and grief. God's command tested the depth of his love, the extent of his faith, and the degree to which he would obey whatever God asked.

A parent can only imagine the feelings that swept through Abraham's heart that night. Yet somehow he moved from shock to the incredible certainty that God's repeated promises regarding Isaac could be trusted. "By faith Abraham, when God tested him, offered Isaac as a sacrifice.... Abraham reasoned that God could raise the dead" (Heb. 11:17-19). Because of his certainty in God's trustworthiness, early the next morning Abraham got up and set out for the place God had told him about (Gen. 22:3). He didn't delay. He didn't try to change God's mind. He quietly and quickly obeyed.

What can we learn from Abraham in this area of quick and willing obedience? First, he didn't stay stuck in the quicksand of his emotions—understandable as that would be. Abraham thought back over what he knew of God's character and the promises He had made. Even as he wrestled with the incompatibility of those promises with God's command, his faith led him to reason out the only answer to his dilemma: Somehow God would raise Isaac from the dead.

When God asks something of us—perhaps to give up an ambition or some right we feel we deserve, to set aside a personal longing, or to find the willingness to humble ourselves and ask for forgiveness— we, too, need to think and reason, drawing on what we know of His character and promises. At the very point of our confusion we must exercise faith in what we believe is true of God. To help you do this, ponder the following statements:

- God loves me and knows what is best.

- God is wiser than I am and can see the future.

- God has loving reasons for what He asks, gives, or withholds.

When God asks something that is costly to you, go through these statements and reason out your feelings and objections in the light of His character. Would God, who is good and loving, ask something of you that is destructive or detrimental? Hardly. What He asks is always for your best, even if it doesn't make sense to you at the moment. Here is where faith must be exercised, with your heart as well as your head. Responding immediately, like Abraham did, shows your conviction that not only is God worthy of your devotion but He is also totally wise. Believing this is essential for growing strong.

Keep Trusting God

When Abraham saw the place God had told him about, he said to his servants, "Stay here ... while I and the boy go over there. We will worship and *then we will come back* to you" (Gen. 22:5).

As father and son walked on together, Isaac asked the question Abraham had been dreading. "Father? ... Where is the lamb for the burnt offering?" And once again we see Abraham's unquestioning faith as he replies with prophetic words, "God himself will provide the lamb for the burnt offering, my son" (Gen. 22:6-8).

Unaware of the full meaning of his words, Abraham pointed to the Lamb of God who would take away the sin of the world. God himself would send His own Son to die on the cross to be a sacrifice for sin—and then raise Him up from the dead.

Abraham loved God enough to offer up his son, picturing thousands of years before Christ the breathtaking truth that "God so loved the world that he gave his one and only Son, that whoever believes in him shall not perish but have eternal life" (John 3:16).

As Abraham took Isaac, his *willing* son, and bound him to the altar, this old man's heart of faith, love, and incredible trust in God's promises and power stood gloriously displayed before the unseen world of demons and angels. Who would not marvel that a human being could love God so supremely that he would offer up what he loved most on earth?

By their actions, both father and son affirmed their heart commitment to the living God. Isaac trusted his father, Abraham, implicitly—and Abraham trusted God with every fiber of his being: "fully persuaded that God had power to do what he had promised" (Rom. 4:21).

Raising his knife, Abraham braced himself to do what God asked—but was stopped midair. A familiar voice called his name, "Abraham! Abraham!"

"Here I am," he replied, hearing the sweetest words he could have hoped for. "Do not lay a hand on the boy ... do not do anything to him" (Gen. 22:11-12). His ordeal was over. Abraham had put God first.

"Worship," says Oswald Chambers, author of the devotional classic *My Utmost for His Highest*, "is giving God the best that He has given you."[4] Abraham shows us the way.

- Was God first in Abraham's life? Absolutely.

- Was Abraham's walk with Him perfect? No.

- Was Abraham a spiritual success in spite of his failures and weaknesses? Yes.

This man, who responded to God's call to leave all that was familiar, who settled down in Haran, who lied about his wife, and who refused to get involved in Sarah's spats with Hagar, nevertheless, by faith believed every promise God gave him. His spiritual journey stands as an exceptional and inspiring example of what God can do with a life fully surrendered to Him.

In explaining the surrendered life, Oswald Chambers says, "True surrender is not simply surrender of our external life but surrender of our will—and once that is done, surrender is complete. Yet God never forces a person's will into surrender, and He never begs. He patiently waits until that person willingly yields to Him. And once that battle has been fought, it never needs to be fought again."[5]

This is the key to walking with God and hearing His "well done."

Daily Choices for the Growing Heart
Live to Hear God's "Well Done"

Living a life that counts for God requires thought and action. Look over these major characteristics of finishing well:

- Maintaining a personal, vibrant relationship with Christ.

- Maintaining a learning posture.

- Showing Christlikeness in your character.

- Living out truth in your life so your convictions and promises are seen to be real.

- Leaving behind a spiritual impact.

Which are present in your life now?

Which do you need to intentionally pursue?

Study Questions

CHAPTER ONE

View Life as an Adventure

Read Hebrews 11:8-19

1. Would you describe your life as a spiritual adventure? Why, or why not?

2. What do you learn about Abraham from these verses? How would you describe him?

3. List the qualities/attitudes you see in Abraham. How did these contribute to his spiritual adventure with God?

4. Which of these qualities or attitudes do you identify with? Which would you like to see developed in your own life? Explain why.

5. Abraham lived "like a stranger in a foreign country" (v. 9). In what ways are Christians in today's culture also strangers in a foreign country? What lessons can you apply from Abraham's example of walking with God regardless of the surrounding culture? (See also Moses' example in vv. 24-27.)

6. Read verses 8-19 again. List the sacrifices that were required of Abraham in one column. In a second column, list the blessings he received from God. What can you learn from this?

7. What repeated word do you find in Hebrews 11? Why doesn't the writer say instead, "By their education, quick wits, courage ..."? What does this teach you about experiencing life as an adventure with God?

8. How has this chapter and Bible study affected the way you look at your life? Is there some new attitude or action you need to put in place as a result? What is it?

9. What new ways of looking at life did you find from reading Ch. One?

CHAPTER TWO

When God Speaks, Say "Yes"

Read Psalm 103

1. Jesus said, "If you love me, you will obey what I command" and "If anyone loves me, he will obey my teaching" (John 14:15, 23). What reasons for loving God do you find in Psalm 103:1-5?

2. How have the benefits listed in verses 3-5 touched and changed your life? What impact does this have on your desire to say yes to what God asks of you?

3. Read verse 6 of the psalm, Isaiah 58:6-10, and Micah 6:8. What impresses you about these verses?

4. List ways people experience oppression today. Might God be nudging you to say yes to Him in regard to those who are oppressed? What small step of obedience can you take to reveal God's heart toward those in need? How will you do this? When will you start?

5. Read verse 7. God spoke to Abraham, made His ways known to Moses, and His deeds to the people of Israel. In what ways has God shown His reality to you?

6. Read verses 8-10. What do you learn of God's character from these verses? How do these statements confirm or contradict your inner feelings and beliefs about God?

7. Read verses 11-17. List the important principles you find about God's love. How do these truths help you?

8. What difference has learning about God's character made in your willingness to do what He asks? How will you put this into practice?

9. How did Ch. Two challenge or inspire you?

CHAPTER THREE

Put Your Faith Into Action

Read James 1:2-4; 2:14-26

1. Reflect on James 1:2-4. How is faith tested?

2. Put in your own words the effect of persevering through a trial. When have you seen this in someone's life?

3. If you're comfortable, share in your study group about a time your faith was tested. What was the result?

4. Read chapter 2:14-18. What do you think these verses mean? How would you apply them to your life? How do they relate to Ephesians 2:8, "By grace you have been saved through faith," and Hebrews 10:38, "My righteous one will live by faith"?

5. God expects faith to result in concern for others, but how else is faith seen and expressed? (Think about your own story, that of others you know, or that of biblical characters.)

6. Read verse 19 of James 2 and Acts 4:12, 33; 17:24-31. What truths about God in these verses encourage you to act on your faith? Be specific.

7. Read verses 20-26. Deeds follow beliefs. What did Abraham believe that enabled him to do what God asked? (Gen. 15:4-6; 22:1-14; Heb. 11:11-12). What did Rahab believe about God that gave her courage to act in faith? (Josh. 2:8-13). What can you learn from this?

8. A growing faith is an essential part of walking with God. For faith to grow, it must be fed. How has a Scripture, the testimony of another person, or a life experience or incident helped to increase your faith?

9. What new insights did you gain about faith from Chapter Three?

CHAPTER FOUR

Count on God's Promises

Read Isaiah 40:28-31; 41:8-10

1. What gives you confidence in the promises of family, friends, or institutions? What takes away your confidence in what they say?

2. In order to count on God's promises, you need to know Him. What does verse 28 of Isaiah 40 tell you about who God is? How does this help you trust His promises?

3. What resources have you found most helpful in increasing your knowledge of God?

4. Read verses 29-31. List the promises given here. Which have you personally experienced? If you're comfortable doing so, briefly share your story.

5. Review Isaiah 41:8-9, and read Ephesians 1:1-14. What
    do you learn about God's heart toward Abraham and his
    descendents? List how God feels toward you as detailed in
    the Ephesians reference. What does this tell you about why
    you can count on His promises?

6. Read Isaiah 41:10 again. What do you think is at the root of
    fear, discouragement, and weakness? How could applying
    the promises in this verse change your perspective and
    attitude toward your difficulties?

7. Reflect on verses 9-10, and then write a thank-you letter to
    God, telling Him what His love and promises mean to you
    and how you will apply them. Share some excerpts with
    one another.

8. How has God encouraged you through this study? Who
    could you encourage by sharing what you have learned?

9. What help did you gain from this chapter on God's
    promises?

CHAPTER FIVE

Trust God in Confusing Circumstances

Read Psalm 23

1. What are the responsibilities of a shepherd? How would a good shepherd feel about his sheep? How would his sheep respond to him?

2. Who is your shepherd? Describe His unique qualities. What makes Him trustworthy?

3. How does the little word *my* encourage you? (v. 1).

4. What "wants" (physical, spiritual, emotional) does the Lord meet? How has He done this in confusing circumstances or in other situations you've faced?

5. Read verse 2 again. Where does the Lord lead His sheep in stressful times? What steps can you take in order to experience this in your life?

6. What does the shepherd do for His sheep? (v. 3). How can you experience this in a situation you face today?

7. List the lessons you find in verse 4. What do they teach you about life, human feelings, and God's presence in painful times? If you're comfortable doing so, share how God helped you through a valley experience.

8. Read verses 5-6 and Hebrews 12:1-3. The outcome of trusting God through difficult circumstances is always an overflowing cup of joy—either in this life or in the Lord's presence forever. What personal help or challenge do you find in Jesus' example of persevering through pain to joy? How can you apply this to your life?

9. What insights encouraged you from reading Ch. Five?

CHAPTER SIX

Consider Conflict as an Opportunity to Grow

Read Romans 12:9-21

1. What effect have you seen conflict have on families, in the workplace, and in the church? (Be discreet in your examples. Don't use names or reveal confidences.)

2. What *attitudes* that contribute to conflict do you find in the following passages: Romans 14:1-4; 10-13; 1 Corinthians 3:1-3; and Galatians 5:19-21?

3. What other attitudes lead to strong disagreements between people? Which do you personally need to watch out for?

4. List the attitudes and actions mentioned in Romans 12:9-21 that would diminish the potential for conflict, if practiced. What can you learn from this?

5. State in your own words what verse 9 means. What does this say about what God wants from you when dealing with a sticky situation or a prickly person?

6. What additional insights do you find in verses 10-16? How can these commands be made practical in your life and current circumstances?

7. Read verses 17-21. How can responding to conflict in a way that pleases God become an opportunity for you to grow spiritually? Try to be specific as you consider both attitudes and actions.

8. How would living according to Romans 12:9-21 affect your relationship with the prickly person(s) in your life? What is God asking you to do in response to His Word?

9. What helped you the most as you read Ch. 6?

CHAPTER SEVEN

Seek to Know the Living God

Read Psalm 63

1. David said to God, "Earnestly I seek you." What are you earnestly seeking in your life—both short-term and long-term?

2. What attitudes and actions are involved in earnestly seeking something you value? How would you apply this to hungering to know God?

3. How would you describe spiritual thirst and weariness? What factors contribute to this experience? If you are comfortable doing so, share about a time in your life when you were in a "dry and weary land" spiritually.

4. List all the antidotes to dryness you find in verses 2-5. Which have you found particularly nourishing to your soul? Why do you think this is true?

5. How does practicing an active praise life increase your awareness of God? What difference could this make in your response to a situation you're currently dealing with?

6. Think about practical ways to stay mentally and spiritually in tune with God. Which could you start practicing today?

7. Read verses 6-8. What actions does David take to show his earnest desire for God? What lessons do you learn from this? How might you apply them to your own life?

8. Look back through chapter 7. How did God challenge you in the area of staying spiritually vibrant? What action will you take to show, like David, your earnest desire for God?

CHAPTER EIGHT

Depend on God's Strength, Not Your Own

Read Acts 16:16-33

1. When have you particularly depended on God's strength? What were the circumstances? What happened as a result?

2. When have you handled a situation in your own strength? What were the results?

3. Read verses 16-18 again. Describe in your own words what was happening. Be honest; how do you think you would have reacted to this irritating situation?

4. What impressed you about Paul's response? How do you see him depending on God's strength, not his own? What can you learn from this for your own life?

5. Review verses 19-31. If you were treated as Paul and Silas were, what would you be feeling, thinking, and saying—to God and to those who harmed you?

6. What were Paul and Silas doing after they were mistreated? How was this possible? What lessons can you apply to yourself from this incident?

7. Read Galatians 2:20 and 5:22-25. How are these truths fleshed out in the response of Paul and Silas to their unfair and brutal treatment? If you feel comfortable doing so, share a time when you responded to a difficult situation in the Spirit rather than in the flesh.

8. Waiting for God to act tests our willingness to depend on Him rather than on ourselves. What practical lessons did you learn in Ch. 8 from the story of Sarah, Abraham, and Hagar about the importance of not running ahead of God? How could you apply this to a situation you're currently facing?

CHAPTER NINE

Turn Failure into a Learning Experience

Read John 4:4-42

1. What makes you feel guilty? What do you tell yourself at these times?

2. How do guilt feelings affect you? What helps you sort through the difference between real and false guilt?

3. Read verses 4-18 again. What does this passage tell you about Jesus? What impresses you about His attitude toward less-than-perfect people? How does it contrast or compare with your own attitude?

4. How would you describe the Samaritan woman? What kind of life do you think she led? What needs did she have? How is she like many women (and men) today?

5. Imagine yourself as the Samaritan woman. How would you feel about yourself? What would be your reaction to Jesus' awareness of your secrets?

6. Read John 8:1-11. What lessons do you learn from Jesus' interaction with both of these women about God's grace for *any* kind of failure in your life?

7. Read Romans 5:6-8 and 1 Peter 2:24. What additional help do you find in these verses for when you fail in the future, or are haunted by guilt feelings from the past? Try to put what these verses are saying into your own words.

8. Review John 4:19-42. List the ways Jesus' grace-filled acceptance of the Samaritan woman impacted her life—inwardly and outwardly. How has His forgiveness and grace toward you affected your life—inwardly and outwardly?

9. What helpful insights into failure, guilt, and grace did you find in Ch.9?

CHAPTER TEN

Live to Hear God's "Well Done"

Read John 11:1-44

1. The differences between Mary and Martha's personalities
    are well known. How would you describe your personality?
    Make five statements reflecting how you see yourself, each
    beginning with the words:

    I am _____.

    I am _____.

    I am _____.

    I am _____.

    I am _____.

2. Why did Mary and Martha send for Jesus? What do you
    think they expected Him to do? How might each of them
    have responded as time went by and Jesus didn't come?

3. Why do you think Jesus didn't go at once? Drawing from the
    whole passage, write down all the ways you see Him using
    this situation to stretch the faith of everyone involved. What
    does this tell you about God's ways in your life?

4. Read verses 21 and 32 again. What same statement
    did Martha and Mary make to Jesus? What were they
    implying? Have you ever felt this way? Share your story, if
    you wish.

5. Read Isaiah 43:1-3, 18-19; 46:4. In times of pain and confusion, what truths about God's compassion, love, and power help you keep pressing toward the goal of hearing "well done, good and faithful servant?" Add other verses that have helped you through difficult times.

6. Review verses 38-40 of John 11. How did Jesus challenge Martha to a new level of faith? How has He done this in your life? Is He challenging you right now? How?

7. What is Jesus' purpose in challenging our faith? (vv. 41-44). What does this teach you about the stretching times God allows in your life?

8. Martha surrendered to the Lord, as did Abraham. What does surrender mean in your life?

9. How might living to hear God's "Well done" make a practical difference in your plans, priorities, and passions?

Notes

Chapter One

1. For the sake of consistency, I have used the names Abraham and Sarah throughout, even though they were first called Abram and Sarai.

2. J. Oswald Sanders, *In Pursuit of Maturity* (Grand Rapids, MI: Zondervan Publishing House, 1986), 14.

Chapter Two

1. Wayne Detzler, *New Testament Words in Today's Language* (Wheaton, IL: Victor Books, 1986), 291.

Chapter Four

1. Wayne Detzler, *New Testament Words in Today's Language* (Wheaton, IL.: Victor Books, 1986), 321.

2. Ibid.

3. F. B. Meyer, *Old Testament Men of Faith* (Westchester, IL: Good News Publishers, 1979), 16.

4. *SIM Now*, Society for International Missions, Fort Mill, South Carolina, issue 90, 6.

Chapter Five

1. Jerry Bridges, *Trusting God* (Colorado Springs, CO: Navpress, 1988), 52.

2. Elisabeth Elliot, *Trusting God in a Twisted World* (Old Tappan, NJ: Fleming H. Revell, 1989), 138-139.

3. Bridges, 46.

4. Arthur W. Pink, *The Attributes of God* (Grand Rapids, MI: Baker Book House, 1975), from the Preface.

Chapter Six

1. Neil S. Wilson, ed., *The Handbook of Bible Application* (Wheaton, IL: Tyndale House Publishers, 1992), 110.

2. Florence Littauer, *The Best of Florence Littauer* (San Bernadino, CA: Here's Life Publishers, 1989), 41.

3. Stuart Briscoe, *Just Between Us* magazine, Fall 2000, 17.

4. Bob Weyant, *Confronting Without Guilt or Conflict* (Belleview, WA: Brassy Publishing, 1994), 2.

Chapter Seven

1. Millard J. Erickson, *Christian Theology*, Second Edition (Grand Rapids, MI: Baker Books, 1998), 296.

2. A. W. Tozer, *The Pursuit of God*, quoted in *Discipleship Journal*, issue 61, 1991, 62.

3. John Piper, *Desiring God* (Portland, OR: Multnomah Books, 1986), 117.

Chapter Eight

1. Neil Anderson & Robert L. Saucy, *The Common Made Holy* (Eugene, OR: Harvest House Publishers, 1997), 160.

2. David Prior, *Living by Faith* (London, UK: Hodder and Stoughton, 1986), 82.

3. Anderson & Saucy, 75, adapted.

4. Anderson & Saucy, 75, adapted.

Chapter Nine

1. Charles Stanley, *In Touch* magazine, August 2000, 9.

2. Amy Carmichael, *Edges of His Ways* (Fort Washington, PA: Christian Literature Crusade, 1975), 119.

3. Gary Collins, *Christian Counseling* (Waco, TX: Word Publishing, 1988), 116.

4. "Marvelous Grace," by Julia H. Johnson.

5. Charles Stanley, *In Touch* magazine, August 2000, 9.

6. Gordon MacDonald, *Rebuilding Your Broken World* (Nashville, TN: Nelson Books, 1990), 203.

Chapter Ten

1. Oswald Chambers, *My Utmost for His Highest* (Grand Rapids, MI: Discovery House Publishers, 1995), reading for May 21.

2. Tony Campolo, quoted by Paul Borthwick, *Six Dangerous Questions* (Downer's Grove, IL: InterVarsity Press, 1996), 119.

3. J. Robert Clinton and Richard W. Clinton, *The Life Cycle of a Leader*, in George Barna, General Editor, *Leaders on Leadership* (Ventura, CA: Regal Books, 1997), 152-153.

4. Chambers, January 6.

5. Ibid., September 13.

Intermedia Publishing Group

Publishing That Works For You

Do you need a speaker?

Do you want Poppy Smith to speak to your group or event? Then contact Larry Davis at: (623) 337-8710 or email: ldavis@intermediapr.com or use the contact form at: www.intermediapr.com.

Whether you want to purchase bulk copies of *Reaching Higher* or buy another book for a friend, get it now at: www.imprbooks.com.

If you have a book that you would like to publish, contact Terry Whalin, Publisher, at Intermedia Publishing Group, (623) 337-8710 or email: twhalin@intermediapub.com or use the contact form at: www.intermediapub.com.